The Economic Crisis and Occupational Stress

NEW HORIZONS IN MANAGEMENT

Series Editor: Professor Sir Cary L. Cooper CBE, *Pro Vice Chancellor for External Relations and Distinguished Professor of Organizational Psychology and Health, Lancaster University, UK and Chair of the Academy of Social Sciences*

This important series makes a significant contribution to the development of management thought. This field has expanded dramatically in recent years and the series provides an invaluable forum for the publication of high quality work in management science, human resource management, organizational behaviour, marketing, management information systems, operations management, business ethics, strategic management and international management.

The main emphasis of the series is on the development and application of new original ideas. International in its approach, it will include some of the best theoretical and empirical work from both well-established researchers and the new generation of scholars.

Titles in the series include:

Psychological Ownership and the Organizational Context
Theory, Research Evidence, and Application
Jon L. Pierce and Iiro Jussila

Handbook of Stress in the Occupations
Edited by Janice Langan-Fox and Cary L. Cooper

The New Knowledge Workers
Dariusz Jemielniak

Narcissism in the Workplace
Research, Opinion and Practice
Andrew J. DuBrin

Gender and the Dysfunctional Workplace
Edited by Suzy Fox and Terri R. Lituchy

The Innovation Imperative in Health Care Organisations
Critical Role of Human Resource Management in the Cost, Quality and Productivity Equation
Edited by Peter Spurgeon, Cary L. Cooper and Ronald J. Burke

Human Resource Management in the Nonprofit Sector
Passion, Purpose and Professionalism
Edited by Ronald J. Burke and Cary L. Cooper

Human Resource Management in the Public Sector
Edited by Ronald J. Burke, Andrew Noblet and Cary L. Cooper

The Psychology of the Recession on the Workplace
Edited by Cary L. Cooper and Alexander-Stamatios G. Antoniou

How Can HR Drive Growth?
Edited by George Saridakis and Cary L. Cooper

Voice and Whistleblowing in Organisations
Overcoming Fear, Fostering Courage and Unleashing Candour
Edited by Ronald J. Burke and Cary L. Cooper

Proactive Personality and Behavior for Individual and Organizational Productivity
Andrew J. DuBrin

Well-being and Beyond
Broadening the Public and Policy Discourse
Edited by Timo J. Hämäläinen and Juliet Michaelson

Competing Values Leadership
Second Edition
Kim S. Cameron, Robert E. Quinn, Jeff DeGraff and Anjan V. Thakor

The Economic Crisis and Occupational Stress
Ritsa Fotinatos-Ventouratos and Cary L. Cooper

The Economic Crisis and Occupational Stress

Professor Ritsa Fotinatos-Ventouratos

Professor of Psychology, Deree College, The American College of Greece, Athens, Greece

Professor Sir Cary L. Cooper CBE

Distinguished Professor of Organizational Psychology and Health, Lancaster University Management School, Lancaster University and Chair of the Academy of Social Sciences, UK

NEW HORIZONS IN MANAGEMENT

 Edward Elgar PUBLISHING

Cheltenham, UK • Northampton, MA, USA

Published by
Edward Elgar Publishing Limited
The Lypiatts
15 Lansdown Road
Cheltenham
Glos GL50 2JA
UK

Edward Elgar Publishing, Inc.
William Pratt House
9 Dewey Court
Northampton
Massachusetts 01060
USA

A catalogue record for this book
is available from the British Library

Library of Congress Control Number: 2014947025

This book is available electronically in the **Elgar**online
Business subject collection
DOI 10.4337/9781781000502

ISBN 978 1 78100 049 6 (cased)
ISBN 978 1 78100 050 2 (eBook)

Typeset by Servis Filmsetting Ltd, Stockport, Cheshire
Printed and bound in Great Britain by T.J. International Ltd, Padstow

Contents

About the authors   vi
Preface   vii
Dedication   ix

PART I ECONOMIC REVIEW

1. Introduction   3
2. The origin of the economic crisis   11
3. Lessons learnt from the past   20

PART II OCCUPATIONAL STRESS IN TIMES OF A CHANGING WORLD

4. The psychological implications of the economic crisis   35
5. The individual and organizational costs of stress   51
6. The consequences of occupational stress in times of a changing
   economic world   76

PART III POST ECONOMIC CRISIS – FROM SUSTAINABILITY TO WELLBEING

7. Organizational effectiveness and wellbeing at work: post
   economic crisis   101
8. Individual and societal wellbeing: an agenda for the future:
   post economic crisis   121

Index   137

About the authors

Professor Ritsa Fotinatos-Ventouratos obtained her Doctorate Degree in Organizational Psychology from UMIST (University of Manchester Institute of Science & Technology), UK. Her areas of research lie in the field of psychological wellbeing at work, occupational stress, gender differences, as well as investigating the social impact on the changing and diverse nature of the world of work. As a professor employed at DEREE College, The American College of Greece, she has been lecturing at this university for over 15 years in the areas of Industrial and Social Psychology. In addition to presenting her research at international congresses and publishing in the domains of work psychology, she serves as a member of the British Psychological Society, International Relations Committee, for the Division of Occupational Psychology.

Professor Sir Cary L. Cooper CBE is Distinguished Professor of Organizational Psychology and Health, and Pro Vice Chancellor at Lancaster University, UK. He is the author/editor of over 120 books (on occupational stress, women at work and industrial and organizational psychology). He was the lead scientist on the UK government's Foresight programme on Mental Capital and Wellbeing, and is a frequent contributor to national newspapers, TV and radio. In 2001, Professor Cooper was awarded a CBE in the Queen's Birthday Honours List for his contribution to occupational safety and health, and in 2007 he was awarded a Lifetime Achievement Award from the Division of Occupational Psychology of the British Psychological Society. He has been an adviser to two United Nations agencies, the World Health Organization and the ILO, and was a special adviser to the Defence Committee of the House of Commons on the Duty of Care enquiry (2004–05). *HR Magazine* named him the second Most Influential UK Thinker in 2013. In 2014 he was awarded a knighthood in the Queen's Birthday Honours List for services to Social Sciences in the context that he has been Chair of the Academy of Social Sciences for a number of years.

Preface

The economic crisis commenced in approximately 2008, when most people around the globe began to learn about two 'failing initiatives'. The first concerned the US mortgage system and housing market, and the second concerned the eurozone and the problematic monetary currency.

Like the majority of people, the authors of this book, who are both psychologists, did not at first pay very much attention to these issues. In fact most people, like us, believed that these problems would soon 'correct themselves' and all would return to equilibrium. Hence, the 'average' citizen went about their normal daily functioning believing this was an 'economic problem' for 'financiers' to correct in the near future. However, it did not take long to realize that we were not suffering from a temporary minor hassle that would correct itself; rather the disruption in economies was a huge and major issue – like an iceberg, where in the beginning we only saw its tip, but underneath was a mighty problem that was about to affect most citizens around the globe, including the working population.

Despite the fact that we, the authors of this book, are not economists, it became apparent to us that people and businesses were heading for a fall and we realized that this would negatively affect people's psychology in the working domain: it almost seemed to us that as one economic change took place so did people's psychology and wellbeing. Thus it was at this point that we decided to venture out and see whether economic problems on the one hand would have, on the other hand, psychological effects in the workplace. Indeed, after tracing and reviewing the economic literature for a long period of time and noticing the peaks and troughs that have taken place throughout history and on a global scale, we can confirm that movements in one sector do have simultaneous movements in the other. Hence, such changes can be reflected, like a mirror, in people's behaviour, in the cognitive thinking strategies, and in the attitudes and overall practices in life. For that reason, we felt it necessary to project these patterns and write this book entitled *The Economic Crisis and Occupational Stress*, where we have systematically analysed and discussed the psychological effects of recessionary periods in the workplace.

It is suggested that the first two parts of this book be viewed as complementary to each other – as one needs to understand the global economic movements (Part I of this book), with the psychological effects on the workplace (Part II). It is in the final part (Part III) that the authors review and recommend suitable coping strategies at the individual, organizational and societal levels.

We hope that by reading this book people will eventually realize, as we did, that economics and psychology are closely matched, like a hand in a glove, and changes in one domain will certainly bring changes in the other. By understanding this process we hope that a coping strategy of awareness will evolve and assist us in moving forward in post-economic crisis eras to sustain wellbeing in the future.

Professor Ritsa Fotinatos-Ventouratos
Professor Sir Cary L. Cooper CBE

Dedication

This book would not be complete if I did not write a few words to the people who supported me throughout this long journey of writing the book. First and foremost to my husband George, who gave me constant encouragement, love and emotional support to see this lifetime achievement met. To my dear children, who for a very long time did not understand what I was doing, and just had the great patience to watch Mum keep writing during weekends, holidays and many early hours of the morning. My dedication also goes to my wonderful Mum, for always listening to me and providing me with an abundance of love and comfort.

I would like to thank my co-author Cary Cooper: spanning over twenty years of knowing each other, he has been my Professor and Supervisor of my Doctorate Degree, teaching me the 'ropes' and expertise of our field and, at the same time, he has been my mentor in academia. Thank you for your words of wisdom, scientific advice and dear friendship.

Professor Ritsa Fotinatos-Ventouratos

I would like to thank Ritsa Fotinatos-Ventouratos for all her kind words and for involving me in the book, a book which means a great deal to her, given the economic problems and stress that Greece has endured over the last six years. Her dedication and persistence has made a significant contribution to understanding how this damaging recession has impacted individuals and businesses throughout the developed world; and, importantly, the health and wellbeing of individuals and their families.

Professor Sir Cary L. Cooper CBE

ACKNOWLEDGEMENTS

More than words of acknowledgment and a thank you to Edward Elgar Publishing, who were spontaneous with suggestions and always full of eagerness to assist with the editing of this book. Francine O'Sullivan,

Jennifer Stanley, Elizabeth Clack, and Yvonne Smith: great to work with all of you!

I would also like to give an acknowledgement and a thank you to the American College of Greece, who has been a solid employer throughout the years. Thank you to my colleagues and my few dear friends in the job; coming to work and seeing smiling faces has greatly helped, and thank you to my long-time friend whom I confided in about this book. Also, an acknowledgment to the staff of the library, who provided me with an abundance of literature whenever I asked. Last, but certainly not least, to my students who have been a total inspiration to me in my 18 years of classroom experience: you have all been a joy to teach.

Professor Ritsa Fotinatos-Ventouratos

PART I

Economic review

1. Introduction

In 1972 when the industrialized world was engaged in a major industrial relations upheaval, Studs Terkel, the social commentator, in his book *Working* (1972), said:

> work is, by its very nature, about violence – to the spirit as well as to the body. It is about ulcers as well as accidents, about shouting matches as well as fistfights, about nervous breakdowns as well as kicking the dog around. It is, above all (or beneath all), about daily humiliations. To survive the day is triumph enough for the walking wounded among the great many of us.

In 2014 we have entered another traumatic time, following the worst global recession in nearly 100 years. The stress levels in the global workplace, and particularly in Europe, are at a very high and unsustainable level, as there are now fewer people in the average workplace, having heavier workloads, feeling job insecure and being more micro-managed than ever before.

Many of us who are reading this book are familiar with the topic of stress at work and acknowledge that there is a plethora of literature available spanning decades of research and covering various issues of occupational stress. Whilst this abundance of literature has proved to be extremely beneficial in past years, it could be suggested that much of it has become outdated due to the rapid economic changes that are currently prevailing on an international scale. Adding to this overall weakness is the failure of the current literature to combine both economic problems and psychological issues under the same umbrella. Unfortunately this means that up until now the two scientific domains have tended to remain separate, with current economic problems being dealt with on the one hand, and psychological work stressors being dealt with on the other. One may speculate that this failure to combine these two scientific fields results in a lack of full understanding and clarity of the current world economic problems, and therefore leads to a lack of insight as to how this adversely affects individuals, organizations and societies at large. It appears that the time has now come for these two spheres to combine as one, since it is evident that the current economic crisis is indeed creating huge psychological changes and impacting on the working lives of all people across the globe. The sheer number of countries, organizations, employees and families who have been negatively affected by this crisis demonstrates the interconnectedness of world economies, human health and overall wellbeing. Therefore, the psychology of people at work in relation to world economies should no longer be seen as separate spheres, but rather as a single entity, tightly interwoven, constituting the realities of all nation states and wellbeing of their people.

Whatever the sector, and whatever the country, it appears that the whole international workforce has been caught up in a kind of tsunami, in the unusual stressors of our current times. This can be clearly seen on a daily basis, as people switch on their televisions and listen to the news, and one is being driven down a road where three specific themes are being constantly addressed, although solutions are yet to be found. These three contemporary themes that we are currently being faced with are: first, the world economic recession that has engulfed the twenty-first century; second, and a knock-on effect from the first (or vice versa), is the overwhelming array of problems in the banking world; and thirdly, and uniquely, is the huge euro crisis stressor, which unfortunately has now turned into a chronic stressor, affecting most eurozone members, and is no longer a unique stressor that we all once believed. The effects of these problems can be seen in a number of ways, which will be discussed further in this book. An example can be seen from figures reported in July 2011 that youth unemployment is widespread in Europe, with figures showing that in the eurozone 20 per cent of those under the age of 25 are out of work, while in Spain the figure is 46 per cent (INSIGHT, 2011). More recently, in March 2014, we learn that unemployment in certain countries, such as Greece, is currently at the particularly high level of 27.5 per cent in the last quarter of 2013, according to the Hellenic Statistical Authority (ELSTAT, March 2014). Moreover and worrisome is the fact that the jobless rate of 27.5 per cent in Q4 2013 was even higher than the Q3 rate of 27 per cent and Q4 rate of 26 per cent recorded in 2012. However, the percentage of the long-term unemployed is at an alarming level, currently standing at 72 per cent, whilst the unemployment rate for young adults (15–24-year-olds) stands at 57 per cent (cited by *Kathimerini* of the *New York Times*, 14 March, 2014). Such figures ultimately imply that there are now fewer people doing more work, and the consequences in terms of stress and health need to be explored.

Coupled with these severe problems are reports emerging indicating that the suicide rates in economically starved Greece, for example, rose by 17 per cent between 2007 and 2009. According to reports based on the World Health Organization and Eurostat figures, Greece has seen the highest increase in suicides over the three-year period, whilst economically troubled Ireland registered the second highest rate at 13 per cent (cited in *Athens News*, September 2011).

These contemporary problems need to be addressed from a combined economic–psychological perspective if appropriate solutions are to be found, and there is a vital need to fully assess and understand the true meaning of global hardship and wellbeing of the world's people. For example, according to NIOSH (2002), as cited in Lundberg and Cooper (2011), during the last couple of decades the workplace in the USA, Europe and some highly developed Asian countries has undergone major changes involving introduction of 'downsizing and outsourcing', 'lean and just-in-time' production, longer working hours and temporary and part-time employment. These changes indeed started as a result of the recession and thereby increased business globalization. The impact on the psychosocial work environment has been higher workloads and greater time pressures (fewer people doing more), increased speed of change, less predictability, decreased job security and job loss.

Corresponding with such economic changes, one should also note that there is a consistent trend in a large part of the globe for stress-related disorders to become more prevalent and severe, and this has been documented for several years now (see, for example, Cooper et al., 2009). For example, data from the Health and Safety Executive (2007) indicate that 420,000 employees in Britain believed they were experiencing stress, depression or anxiety at levels that were making them ill. Furthermore, the World Health Organization (2001) identified mental health problems and stress-related disorder as 'the biggest overall cause of early death in Europe'. Similarly and according to the European Working Conditions Survey 2006 (cited in Lundberg and Cooper, 2011), 30–40 per cent of workers reported such problems, with the highest figures in the new member states.

Additionally, in the UK stress has been estimated to cost the economy between 5 and 10 per cent of GNP per annum (see Table 1.1; Cooper, 2005) and mental illnesses (e.g. depression, chronic fatigue syndrome, anxiety, personality disorders, drug abuse problems, schizophrenia) and pain problems are the most common reasons for individuals describing their state of health as 'poor'.

At the same time and of concern is the emergence of different economic and employment patterns, and as economic analysis of future employment patterns by Oxford Economics suggests: 'We may expect to see a gradual rise in reports of stress, depression and anxiety over the coming years, as employment shifts towards professional and service occupations where the prevalence of stress, depression and anxiety is reportedly higher' (cited in Dewe et al., 2010).

Table 1.1   The costs of workplace stress and mental health problems in the UK

1. Total cost to employers of mental ill-health at work is estimated at £29.5 billion per annum[1]
2. Stress from work per annum costs employers an estimated £3.7 billion[2]
3. 13 million working days are lost[3]
4. Total cost of incapacity benefit per annum is £12 billion[4]
5. Nearly 40% of people drawing incapacity benefit (IB) have a mental health condition = £5 billion

Cost of stress in the workplace results from a wide range of sources such as:

● sickness absence;
● labour turnover;
● premature retirement;
● health insurance;
● treatment of consequences of stress.

Notes:
1. Sainsbury Centre for Mental Health (2008).
2. Confederation of British Industry (CBI) (2005).
3. Health and Safety Committee (HSC) (2004).
4. Department for Work and Pensions (DWP) (2006).

Source: Lundberg and Cooper (2011). *Government Office for Science*, Department for Innovation, Universities and Skills (DIUS).

It appears, therefore, that the current global economic crisis has brought about a host of problems and transformations, with major repercussions being felt at personal, organizational and societal levels.

Furthermore, and in recent years, we have seen great changes in working conditions in industrialized countries, related to a more global economy and advanced technologies that have given rise to more competition around the world, increased demands for speed, greater efficiency and productivity, and a faster pace of work. In the more recently developed and emerging countries, such as China, South Korea and India, these changes have been even faster and more dramatic, and hence are most likely to cause stress for people in these countries. Additionally, and as stated by Lundberg and Cooper (2011), repeated economic recessions such as the current one that we are experiencing have contributed to additional turbulence and have intensified the restructuring of companies and manufacturing innovation, leading ultimately to reduction of personnel. Furthermore, and as has been evident in recent years, such changes will be followed by increased unemployment and even higher demands on the remaining employees. Demands for more advanced training and education and a faster pace of work make it almost impossible for people without these qualifications to obtain permanent work. Adding to these problems are other social and economic issues that need to be discussed, such as pension cuts as a result of this recession and the collapse of the banking sector, which ultimately means that people will need to work longer and harder, with consequent implications across many societies. It seems, therefore, and without a doubt that organizations, whatever their size and however they may be structured, are not immune from economic, social and psychological turmoil. As we will discuss throughout this book, government initiatives, regulations and appropriate management practices need to be put in place to help alleviate the work stressors that are being encountered during this economic world crisis.

Further reasons for the escalating world problems and transformations taking place are a result of the fact that during the past century, the life and identity of contemporary man has been grounded on a society that has advertised employment, consumption and financial status as its primary motives and top priority needs. As beautifully pointed out in the early 1950s by the famous sociologist Maria Jahoda (1958), our employment status signifies to the outside world our 'identity': the 'who I am' construct. Suddenly today, we are having to educate our people that it is the opposite: we are in reverse gear, and we are having to contend with fewer jobs, fewer employment prospects, and much less income to consume; hence our society no longer can be built on the foundation of consumption and financial and employment status. These unique stressors of our current times are not only reflecting practical issues, but equally important 'symbolic' ones, which are tapping into a wide range of psychological issues that vitally need to be addressed. It must therefore be realized amongst laymen and professionals alike that this global economic crisis is adversely affecting most individuals in some form, causing multiple upheavals for individuals, organizations and community-wide functioning, the repercussions of which we are just beginning to see. Against the backdrop of these negative occupational, economic, social and political problems, we identify a number of societal issues reflecting discontent. It might be predicted that rising crime statistics reflect this discontent and also the motivation to find immediate gratification through unlawful means of income. Indeed, according to Weinberg and Cooper (2012), it has been suggested that there are indications on both sides of the Atlantic that this may be true. Within the United Kingdom, different statistics emerge from the police and the British Crime Survey, with the latter showing that domestic burglary had increased by 14 per cent between 2009 and 2011 (Home Office/ONS, 2011, cited in Weinberg and Cooper 2012). Personal and household crimes in the United Kingdom – including theft of unattended property from gardens and businesses, as well as personal items left unguarded, such as wallets – also increased by 10 per cent. A similar pattern emerged in the United States, with the estimated rate of burglaries increasing by 2 per cent over the five-year period of 2005–09 (FBI, 2009, cited in Weinberg and Cooper, 2012). It could be suggested (despite the vagueness of interpreting such statistical data across countries) that in times of economic recession, societies are paying dearly in terms of petty theft and burglaries within communities and against fellow citizens.

Naturally, therefore, it is important that a full examination of the correct management of economic and social issues is needed, and these contemporary problems need to be addressed from a combined economic–psychological perspective if appropriate solutions are to be found. A large body of research is able to show that there is a strong connection between human health and the work environment, although professionals acknowledge that there is often a time-lag between the experience of stress and the onset of medical symptoms (Theorell, 1998). Given that the impact of the economic crisis is still in full swing, it seems appropriate to suggest that the time has now come to fully assess its impact in both economic and psychological terms.

Furthermore and coupled with these severe problems is the enormous obstacle that there are no lessons from the past, regarding the euro crisis, that can guide any economist or government in finding a workable solution. This is due to the unique nature of the euro, 'the experiment that once was' in the beginning of the twenty-first century. This of course means that unlike in the past, there are no quick remedies, there are no quick solutions, and there are no economic models or theories that can be reapplied to today's crisis. Our contemporary problems for all, both employees and employers, for economists, governments and occupational psychologists, are being tested and tried for the first time in an attempt to find expert solutions. It also seems thus far that professional sectors are generally working alone and not in tandem, each seeking to find a solution to the escalating world economic problems.

Resulting in the lack of current remedies available, this has allowed each and every one of us to portray these international problems through our own individual lens, and each person, whether professional or layman, is seeking a justification for their views. The euro crisis, therefore, has become a popular topic of conversation, almost fashionable to discuss amongst friends, politicians, economists or even strangers meeting on the bus to go to work. The eurozone has even become a popular topic of conversation amongst friends in different countries whereby, when meeting, their common thread and introductory topic is 'how is your country coping with the euro in comparison to our country?' It is a well known fact, however, that underlying such confusion of thought and ambiguity is an abundance of strong theoretical and research findings by psychologists (see, for example, Karasek, 1990; Cooper, 1988; Fotinatos-Ventouratos and Cooper, 1998), which confirms that uncertainty in itself and hence lack of control is a huge psychological stressor.

If the general population had known in advance that the euro and the impact of the economic crisis had an 'expiry date', then this by itself may have added a 'psychological safety net' for the average employee and employer to have in the back of their minds as a coping strategy. If they had been assured that the problem would end, albeit in the long term, appropriate psychosocial counter-measures could have been taken. But this is not the case, and today's issues are very different from any other time in the past, and the stressors and strains of our contemporary times need to be addressed and dealt with in an exceptionally unique one-off time. It could be suggested, therefore, that in order to fully comprehend our combined work and economic problems in the twenty-first century, there is a need to have an 'eye on the past', an 'eye on the present', and a solid vision for the future. Therefore, in order to accurately address our contemporary problems, it is necessary to trace our very recent past and to shed accurate light on how we have reached where we are today, in a world of combined economic crisis and workplace upheaval, to find feasible solutions for us all.

This is exactly what we have attempted to do in compiling this book. The book is divided into three parts as we look at the past and present and have a picture for the future. More analytically: Part I of this book, therefore, addresses the economic position of this crisis and reflects on the historic past, to give the reader an insight into how we came to where we are today, with the economic problems and effects of globalization. In Part II of this book, we analytically describe the psychological impact of this economic crisis, and this is assessed at both the individual and organizational level. The consequences of this economic crisis in terms of occupational stress are discussed separately in Chapter 6, where we will highlight the ongoing stressors in the changing turbulent world of work. The final, third part of this book, chapters 7 and 8, addresses the issues of wellbeing at work in the post-economic crisis era and an evaluation is given in terms of both organizational effectiveness and individual and societal wellbeing, with a vision for a healthier and psychologically more stable future.

REFERENCES

Athens News (2011). Youth unemployment suicide rates, *Athens News*, 23 September, available at: www.athensnews.gr.

Cooper, C.L. (1988). *Theories of Organizational Stress*. Oxford: Oxford University Press.

Cooper, C.L. (2005). *Handbook of Stress, Medicine and Health*, 2nd edn. Boca Raton, FL: CRC Press.

Cooper, C.L., Field, J., Goswami, U., Jenkins, R. and Sahakian, B. (eds) (2009). *Mental Capital and Wellbeing*. Oxford: Wiley-Blackwell.

Dewe, P.J., O'Driscoll, M.P. and Cooper, C.L. (2010). *Coping with Work Stress. A Review and Critique*. Chichester: Wiley-Blackwell.

Fotinatos-Ventouratos, R.S.J. and Cooper, C.L. (1998). Social class differences and occupational stress. *International Journal of Stress Management*, 5(4), 211–22.

Health and Safety Executive (2007). *Violence at Work*. London: HSE.

Hellenic Statistical Authority (HSE) (ELSTAT) (2014). National Statistical Service of Greece: Division of Statistical Information and Publication, 21 March.

INSIGHT (October 2011). Economic Research and Investment Strategy, Gary Shilling's INSIGHT, XXVII (10), available at: www.agaryshilling.com.

Jahoda, M. (1958). *Current Concepts of Positive Mental Health*. New York: Basic Books.

Karasek, R.A. (1990). Lower health risk with increased job control among white-collar workers. *Journal of Occupational Behaviour*, 11, 171–85.

Kathimerini (2014). Jobless rate at 27.5 percent in Oct–Dec, *International Herald Tribune*, English edn, 14 March, available at: www.ekathimerini.com.

Lundberg, U. and Cooper, C.L. (2011). *The Science of Occupational Health: Stress, Psychobiology and the New World of Work*. Chichester: Wiley-Blackwell.

Terkel, S. (1972). *Working*. New York: Avon Books.

Theorell, T. (1998). Stress on the Job: The future of work and its relationship to human health. *Scandinavian Journal of Work, Environment & Health*, Supplement no. 4. Available at: http://www.nnn.se/archive/stress.htm.

Weinberg, A., and Cooper, C.L. (2012). *Stress in Turbulent Times*. Basingstoke: Palgrave Macmillan.

World Health Organization (WHO) (2001). *The World Health Report 2001: Mental Health: New Understanding, New Hope*. Geneva: WHO.

2. The origin of the economic crisis

In order to assess the psychological impact of the economic crisis, it is essential to take one step back and shed light on how we have reached where we are today. By getting to grips with the origin of this global crisis and by fully understanding various world events that unfolded, a greater and more solid vision can be established. This is necessary because any world economic crisis not only means economic misfortune, but also psychological turbulence in the world of work occurs simultaneously. It could be suggested that at the most superficial level, the rate of growth of any economy is by definition the sum of productivity growth *and* workforce growth, the latter of which appears to have been neglected or pushed aside dramatically in this current world recession. However, beginning nearly two centuries ago, the true determinants of economic growth were outlined in the Primitive Production Function model (as cited in Strategic Economic Decisions, 2010), which clearly included the workforce as a key determinant factor in the equation. More specifically, the output of an economy began to be interpreted via a simple theory in which existing technology transformed the three basic factors of production into output. These three 'input' factors were land, workforce and capital. In compact form this can be written as follows:

$$Y = F(L, W, C) + e$$

Where Y denotes output, F is the 'production function' or technology that transforms inputs into outputs, L is land, W is workforce, C is capital and e is adjustment factors (this formula is based on the original work cited in Strategic Economic Decisions, 2010).

Obviously, the scope of this book is primarily to examine the W in the equation, but it can clearly be seen that all variables are tightly interwoven, and therefore should be assessed and recognized in this format. In particular this model tells us that the more land or workers a nation has, the greater will be its growth and economic power. However, if we are to take this basic theoretical model and reflect it on the current economic issues prevailing, one may see that there is a huge gap and underutilization of this model. Moreover, figures from the OECD and ILO have already warned that the jobless from the 2007–09 span of recession are currently estimated at 20 million in the G-20 group, which is a devastatingly high figure to contend with (Economic Research Investment Strategy, 2011).

Unemployment is one immediate and critical problem that can be visibly seen and assessed for any economic crisis; however, in this current twenty-first century recession, a host of different issues ranging from and including: job insecurity, psychological ill-health, occupational stress, sharpening of global competition, and growing tension and conflict amongst workers are but a few critical variables that need to be examined further on. At this point, however, an account of how the recent trends unfolded on an international scale is presented below, the impact of which can be evaluated subsequently in the following chapter.

THE CRISIS IN THE UNITED STATES

This current economic crisis began in the United States with the mortgage meltdown around 2006 (Friedman, 2011). To be more accurate, it originated in a financial system whereby paper assets were generated whose value depended on the price of the housing. The general assumption behind these paper assets was that the price of homes would always rise, and at the very least, if the price fluctuated the value of the paper could always still be determined. Unfortunately, neither of these two assumptions proved to be true and this created huge instability in reality and also in the perception of people's minds. The consequences that followed were that the price of housing in the United States declined and the value of the paper assets could not be determined (see Figure 2.1). Ultimately this placed the entire American financial system in gridlock, and the crisis spilled over into Europe, where many financial institutions had also purchased the paper.

More analytically, the roots of this economic and financial crisis tell us that during economic expansions, financial investors may aim to find investments that generate large returns, although at times this means that they send their money after rather risky prospects. One of the most important of these investments in recent years was indeed the subprime mortgages in the United States, which culminated in mortgage loans that recklessly required minimal to non-existent credit checks, minimum down payments and sometimes no proof of income at all, accumulating in some $550 billion of subprime loans (cited STRATFOR, 10 October 2008). It may be suggested that whilst this action created huge financial problems in the economic world, the psychological impact for the average person

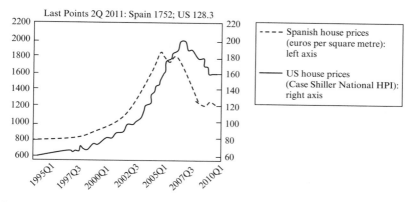

Source: Standard & Poor's and Bank of Spain.

Figure 2.1 House prices in USA and Spain (2011)

was detrimental, and the adverse consequences are still to be determined by organizational and health specialists.

Coupled with the above economic and financial losses, there was a further obstacle: specifically, mortgages are only rarely kept by their issuers, instead they are bundled into packages, known as securitization, and sold to the interested investors to serve three purposes. First, since the mortgage maker can sell the loan for a profit, he/she is then in a position to make another mortgage. Second, this secondary tier of investors brings an entirely new source of capital into the market, and thirdly, these packaged mortgages can be sold to yet more investors, thus creating a new series of mortgage-backed assets that can be traded abroad. Taken together, this widens and deepens the capital pool and reduces mortgage rates for everyone. And this is exactly the procedure that prevailed a few years ago, which eventually created havoc in the financial and economic world. Investors and market players chased after ever-shrinking returns and nobody questioned the dubious mortgages as anything different from normal mortgages – and that included the rating agencies, whose job it was to evaluate products! (cited STRATFOR, 10 October 2008). It took some time for economists, financiers and politicians to understand the magnitude of this problem and all failed to take responsibility for the loss incurred and, frankly, durable recovery became a myth.

Ultimately, all banks and investment houses are required to retain a percentage of their assets in hard cash so as not to become overleveraged. This reserve percentage is based upon many factors, but an important one is the risk of the investments. Until now, mortgage investments were considered in the 'mind' of others as safe investments, because homeowners will do everything they can to avoid missing payments and ultimately feeling insecure and anxious that they may lose their home. However, the financial and economic game went exceptionally wrong and many people were suddenly faced with the reality of home losses, overriding debts that could not be paid, and organizational problems emerged in the form of job insecurity and job losses that became a living tragedy.

In summary, it became a misguided trend for all types of people, in any socio-economic status and without any financial proof of income to request a mortgage. The resulting fact was that many of these mortgages were granted without requiring down payments so no equity was ever earned and the subprime mortgages fell into default. Eventually and in simplistic terms, investors suddenly found themselves having to use cash reserves to cover up and rebalance their paper asset sheets. Finally, as the house prices dropped precipitously in the United States, investors all over the world who might have once been willing to purchase or trade these mortgage-backed securities lost interest and had no psychological trust in such investments, and the unlucky holders held assets of questionable value that could not be unloaded. The results were twofold: (1) due to this economic crisis in the United States, the world saw the cash crunch of firms increase and investment houses started to break apart; and (2) in the world of work we saw the consequences of this economic crisis adversely affect the workforce in a host of ways, ranging from severe occupational stress, job insecurity and various other struggles related to downsizing and restructuring on the economic platform.

Furthermore and as a conclusion to the economic crisis in America, it should be noted that unlike banks, the major investment houses in the United States are regulated by the Securities and Exchange Commission instead of the Treasury – and are only required to set aside a minimum amount of cash. This amounted to less than 1 per cent of their total asset list and provided them with a much smaller cushion than the banks held. The end result was that by September 2008 major Wall Street investment houses such as Lehman Brothers and Bear Stearns had gone bankrupt. In less than six months, the financial world in America had erupted and everything on Wall Street changed, sending shock waves across Europe and other world nations.

THE CRISIS IN EUROPE

The American economic crisis impacted Europe almost immediately, causing chaos in the banking world, investment world and soon after hitting both the public and private working sectors in most European countries. All areas of modern day work have been affected and people of all socio-economic status and in all forms of employment have felt the shockwaves of this economic crisis. Whilst there are similarities and differences between the European and American crises, it must be recognized that for Europe there has been the additional unique problem of the eurozone invention, which has created numerous difficulties for today's working population in most countries. It has become apparent that the nature of jobs has now changed dramatically, different countries and organizations have become constrained, and greater unemployment and job insecurity have predominated, making the fewer people left in the employment arena very vulnerable and forced to work unrealistically long hours. The consequences of this economic crisis (to be discussed in later chapters) have now spilled over in the home domain, in addition to giving rise to social unrest in some countries. For example, public disturbances in reaction to fiscal restraints have occurred amongst the normally super-reserved British and this is especially so among public sector employees who face layoffs, pay cuts, higher contributions to their pension funds and later retirements.

More specifically, the origin of this economic crisis began in Europe due to a variety of combining factors, including the American mortgage meltdown (discussed previously), which sent ripple effects across the European banking sector, causing write downs and credit losses, in addition to the common European currency, which appears still today to have failed miserably. Taking a look back at how we got to where we are today, it must be remembered that the Maastricht Treaty was first signed in 1992, when EU member states agreed to form a common currency. This forming of a common currency originally seemed a positive move for all; however, it certainly did not consider two vitally important issues: the implications of the world of work (the W mentioned in our original model), incorporating labour costs and employment contracts in each country, and secondly, the fiscal integration and business cycles of the different EU member states. Thus by forming a common currency, without fiscal integration, the business cycles of the countries involved were unable to work in synchrony and labour imbalances and terms of conditions became unequally transferable from country to country.

These major undetected obstacles were initially hidden and the rush to a common currency took place. The subsequent economic growth of the early 2000s hid a myriad of eurozone problems and inconsistencies, with huge differences in work ethics and labour structures, which soon rose to the surface. Today, for example, Germany's labour unit costs have risen by 6 per cent since the advent of the euro, but jumped by 20 per cent in France, 33 per cent in Italy, 34 per cent in Ireland, 36 per cent in Spain, and 41 per cent in Greece (Insight, August 2011). Not unexpectedly, and simultaneously, confidence amongst both consumers and businesses in the eurozone has now dramatically fallen as manufacturers' export orders fall and consumers are worried about a hopelessly deteriorating job market. In retrospect, therefore, the eurozone has not created a unified Europe, as was its aim; rather it has encouraged huge divergences on an economic scale, and huge imbalances and disruption in the labour force of most European countries.

Starting with the imbalances on an economic and financial platform, Table 2.1, taken from the Bank for International Settlements (2011), shows the sheer and *varying* amount of monies that were needed to 'rescue' certain countries by the end of 2010, in terms of foreign exposure.

Moving on with the above information in mind, it is clear that this recession has generated a *disproportionate* economic crisis in certain European countries, such as Greece, Spain, Portugal and Ireland, and at the same time this has created *disproportionate* work and organizational problems. More specifically youth unemployment is horrendously widespread in Europe, with 20 per cent of those under 25 in the eurozone out of work, and 46 per cent in Spain (Insight, August 2011). Additionally, Irish unemployment stood at a serious high of 13.5 per cent as early as 2010, and the ongoing trend unfolding in Ireland is to see an exodus of people, including many educated individuals, previous homeowners and Ireland's skilled workforce, emigrating to other homelands. Furthermore, problems are magnified in countries with slow economic growth, which are primarily those countries with rigid labour markets and that are unable to adjust wages for worker productivity. In contrast, other European countries, the Netherlands for example with 7.1 per cent of youth unemployment, and Austria with 8.2 per cent are better equipped and have specialized training programmes geared to job openings (Friedman, 2011). In summary therefore, the origins of this economic crisis have certainly demonstrated the

Table 2.1   Foreign exposure to Greece, Ireland, Portugal and Spain by bank nationality, end 3Q 2010, US$ billion

	Germany	France	UK	Japan	US	R.O.W.	Total
Greece	69.4	92.0	20.4	2.0	43.1	51.0	277.9
Ireland	208.3	78.1	224.6	22.5	113.9	166.4	813.7
Portugal	48.5	45.6	33.7	2.8	47.1	144.3	321.8
Spain	242.4	224.7	152.4	29.2	187.5	262.7	1098.8
Total	568.6	440.4	431.1	56.5	391.6	624.4	2281.3

Source: Bank for International Settlements (2010), cited in INSIGHT (October, 2011).

strong negative associations that have simultaneously occurred within the labour force. It can be stated with confidence that such extreme economic turbulence experienced in Europe will certainly continue to manifest itself in a deterioration of both physical and psychological wellbeing in the world of work, and this will be examined fully in subsequent chapters.

THE CRISIS IN CHINA

The origins of the American and European crises had undoubtedly strong effects in China, which today is still considered the number one export economy (STRATFOR, August 2011). It was exactly this 'exporting' factor that directly affected China, sending into turbulence a nation's workforce which is primarily regulated by the Chinese government. For example, copper prices went down 28 per cent, but dropped 60 per cent between July and December 2008 as the recession in China also unfolded (Friedman, 2011). More specifically, it must be stated that as soon as America and Europe went into economic recession, the demand for Chinese exports from these two world areas slumped drastically, and eventually the Chinese government was faced with a dilemma on how to re-stabilize an employment crisis that was to erupt in this country. Quite frankly, the government was faced with two options: either it had to immediately close leading industries and factories within the country, although this would have devastating consequences on the world of work, or the second option was to keep industries running, but by forcing strict price reductions. The former option would entail a direct consequence of people losing their jobs and the risk of social unrest would be high; the second option would again have negative implications for the wellbeing of the worker in terms of profit margins deteriorating to nearly zero per cent, and hence a huge reduction in salaries would be requested. As other world economies watched China from a distance, it became apparent that the second option was the primary one chosen by the Chinese government, but at the cost of soaring inflation throughout China. It did not take long for the mediating effects of job stress and reduced job involvement to set in, and the resulting job instability also occurred in many employment sectors, including the most traditional banking service personnel of Taiwan (Ouyang, 2009).

In summary therefore, it soon became apparent that China had been caught up in this depression, but with one more severe and additional problem to contend with: China currently does not have a welfare state programme in practice, and understandably the insecurity that entailed for all people in this nation accelerated. The current results are that the workforce has been hit by inflation, and both consumers and businesses in the long run have had their interests and exports affected, resulting in fewer competitive and profitable businesses, and for employees the ultimate blow has been a huge reduction in salaries too. In conclusion, therefore, like most other nation states, China was faced with a huge economic crisis that adversely impacted at the individual, organizational and societal level.

OTHER NATIONS

It should be mentioned that not every country is considered to be experiencing this current economic crisis and therefore some world sectors

Table 2.2   Government debt as a percentage of GDP

	1980	1990	2000	2010
United States	46	71	58	97
Japan	53	66	145	213
Germany	31	42	61	77
United Kingdom	58	42	54	89
France	34	46	73	97
Italy	54	93	126	129
Canada	71	109	115	113
Australia	43	46	37	41
Austria	36	59	76	82
Belgium	61	140	121	115
Denmark	36	77	73	65
Finland	16	23	67	57
Greece	26	83	124	132
Netherlands	65	97	67	76
Norway	43	38	44	65
Portugal	36	68	63	107
Spain	27	49	71	72
Sweden	58	54	77	58
Totals of above				
Median	43	63	72	97
Weighted average	46	66	78	104
Simple average	44	67	81	93
G-7	50	67	90	107
Other advanced	41	67	75	85
Memo: Std deviation	15	29	31	29

Source: Bank for International Settlements (2011).

are not facing the unique stressors that have been outlined above. For example, Russia indeed went through an economic crisis several years ago, and Brazil and India have not experienced the extremes of China, although it must be acknowledged that the latter two countries have not had the extreme growth rates of China either. Moreover, Table 2.2 highlights government debt in various countries as a percentage of GDP, and here the high trends in countries such as the United States and various European countries such as Portugal and France should be noted. Therefore and in conclusion, it can be said with great confidence that when the United States, China and Europe enter such a crisis, this should not be considered a trivial event for any country, employee or employer across the globe, and it is apparent that the stressors that we are facing are both severe and unique and need to be further explored in the forthcoming chapters of this book.

REFERENCES

Bank for International Settlements (BIS) (2011). The real effects of debt, Working Paper No. 352, September, BIS.

Friedman, G. (2011). Global economic downturn: a crisis of political economy, STRATFOR, 9 August, available at: http://www.stratfor.com.

INSIGHT (August 2011). Economic Research and Investment Strategy, Gary Shilling's INSIGHT, XXVII (8), available at: www.agaryshilling.com.

INSIGHT (October 2011). Economic Research and Investment Strategy, Gary Shilling's INSIGHT, XXVII (10), available at: www.agaryshilling.com.

Ouyang, Y. (2009). The mediating effects of job stress and job involvement under job instability: Banking service personnel of Taiwan as an example. *Journal of Money, Investment and Banking*, 11, 16–26.

Strategic Economic Decisions (2010). 'The rise of the East, and the decline of the West' – A clarification of what this really means, H.R. Brock, available at: www.sedinc.com.

STRATFOR (10 October 2008). The financial crisis in the United States, editor's note, 10 October, STRATFOR Global Intelligence, available at: www.stratfor.com.

STRATFOR (13 October 2008). The financial crisis in Europe, editor's note, 13 October, STRATFOR Global Intelligence, available at: www.stratfor.com.

STRATFOR (9 February 2010). Germany's choice, Marko Papic and Peter Zeihan, 9 February, STRATFOR Global Intelligence, available at: www.stratfor.com.

3. Lessons learnt from the past

The aim of the previous chapter was to draw attention to the origins of the economic crisis and highlight the various global problems that have been created. The objective of this chapter is twofold: first, it is necessary to assess whether various scientists, governments and official bodies were aware that such a recession would occur, and if so, why were preventative measures not taken? And secondly, if such a crisis was inevitable and known, what lessons, if any, have been learnt from the past? This chapter is primarily an economic review of historical events, which may indeed resemble the current economic crises being experienced and the consequences thereof. Although economically driven, such information is needed in order to fully examine the 'W' component of our model (that is, the workforce), which we discussed earlier, which is of primary concern to industrial/organizational psychologists. It is natural to suggest that in order to evaluate whether any lessons have been learnt from the past, one must be aware of what history reveals in terms of previous economic crises. History acts as a pointer; as the old saying goes, 'history repeats itself', so we need to put this crisis in some kind of historical perspective.

One could start off by saying that all economic crises of any shape and form are considered 'rare events', otherwise the word 'crisis' would not be a justifiable term. Whatever its shape and form, a world economic crisis appears to have two components: first, it is something that is probably 'unpredictable', at least to the general public, and secondly, it is 'damaging' for the people and countries who are involved. On a social psychological front, it seems that economic crises have the impact of breaking down 'what we are' and change 'what we know', creating a new alloy of people and societies that eventually rest on the new economic foundations laid after a given crisis. For the W component, the employment sector is directly hit as job losses soar, and income in the world is directly reduced due to a host of factors, ranging from a decline in production and manufacturing, servicing and economic activity of all kinds. Here we see that those left in the employment arena are faced with wage cuts and simultaneous tax rises, and greater input in 'manpower' hours at work is often requested. Given the fact that all economies of all sizes, and all nations both rich and poor, work on the elements of buying and selling products, a world recession involves problems in the simple equation of buy and sell, which ultimately affects governments and banks internationally and hits the world of work and its people in many negative ways.

Whilst it has been suggested above that economic crises are 'rare' events, they certainly are not unheard-of phenomena and indeed economic crises have been discussed in both fictional and non-fictional contexts in the past. For example, going back many years, the readers of this book will probably remember the classic film entitled *Mary Poppins*. In this film we are led to believe that banks had lost money through gambling schemes and furthermore that the banks were not able to pay off panicked depositors, who came to collect their monies. Even though this classic film is fictional, the theme of *Mary Poppins* certainly appears to have been rooted in reality. Today such events are commonly referred to as 'banking runs' and periodically during history such events unfold (for example, in the United Kingdom with the well-known building society Northern Rock in 2007) (Reinhart and Rogoff, 2009). Moving on to a historical terminology trace, the word 'unemployment' is a term that came into common use in the late nineteenth century (Olson, 1982), and this can possibly imply to us that economic turmoil which eventually creates unemployment is certainly well embedded in our history.

At a glance therefore, one may suggest then that the phenomenon of 'not working' is certainly not new, and indeed it is firmly rooted in history, although it is further necessary to review the reasons *why* unemployment has occurred and *when* an economic crisis is likely to unfold, as looking at analogies is an essential first step. It must be remembered from the previous chapter that crises can be triggered by a host of issues but primarily it seems that two sources prevail that lead to nations falling into debt or experiencing an 'economic crisis' as the factual term states. The first is through excessive *private or public sector borrowing*, which often looks like a binge phenomenon, and therefore inflates housing and stock prices and makes the economy seem more stable and profitable than it really is, and secondly, this may cause *banking crises*, which affect all nations, rich and poor. So it seems that when countries become indebted for either of the above two reasons, they are heading for trouble and economic default may occur. Although these types of scenarios are not every day events, over the long course of history such economic problems are bound to develop; the exact timing perhaps can be very difficult to estimate, but nonetheless, a crisis will eventually ignite!

In a wonderful book entitled *This Time is Different*, the authors, Reinhart and Rogoff (2009), describe to the reader that 'debt crises' have ranged from those related to the mid-fourteenth century loans by Florentine financiers to England's Edward III, to German merchant bankers' loans to Spain's Habsburg monarchy, and to massive loans made by New York bankers to Latin America during the 1970s! Indeed, in its early years as a nation state France defaulted on its external debt no fewer than eight times, Spain defaulted a mere six times prior to 1800, but with seven defaults in the nineteenth century. Furthermore, and of historical concern, is that from 1800 until after World War II, Greece found itself virtually in continuous default, and furthermore Greece's default in 1826 shut it out of international capital markets for 53 consecutive years. Shedding more light on lessons learnt from the past, it has further been documented (Reinhart and Rogoff, 2009) that throughout history numerous defaults occurred in France, Portugal, Prussia, Spain and the early Italian city states. At the edge of Europe, moreover, Egypt, Russia and Turkey also have histories of chronic default. In a recent article (Mauldin, 2012), it has been cited that Habsburg Spain defaulted on all or part of its debt fourteen times between 1557 and 1696, and also succumbed to inflation due to a surfeit of New World silver, whilst Portugal has defaulted on its national debt five times since 1800, and overall there have been an outstanding total of more than 250 sovereign debt defaults since 1800!

Given such information, it can confidently be suggested that when today's European powers began to consider our possible investment in the eurozone adventure, a closer look at historical events may have been beneficial to all. Certainly, the history of economic debt seems to have been largely ignored, whilst it is this exact issue that needs to be focused on when looking at a historical pattern: we ultimately need to learn from our past, in order to have a vision for the future.

It must also be acknowledged that whilst an individual's private economic problems and debt are a worrying state of affairs, it must be recognized that government debt seems to be a fundamental characteristic of whether a nation and its economy will experience a recession. Thus, the financial status of any government appears to be a common denominator in assessing whether an economic crisis may develop. It seems, however, that such *factual* government information is often difficult to find, and hence trying to obtain a true picture of where nations stand on an economic front is almost impossible, often until a problem is exposed. The recent and current economic crisis in Greece, for example, may be explained by the contributing factor that the Greek government not only hid financial data from the outside world, but furthermore, the figures that were eventually presented were not the true ones. One may argue that if government data is not presented in a crystal clear manner, then appropriate financial predictions surely cannot be made. Here one may resort to the old saying that 'prevention is better than cure', and having transparent data readily available would without any doubt assist in detecting economic problems in their infancy. For example, evidence shows (Reinhart and Rogoff, 2009) that in the 1990s over 45 nation states had an extraordinarily high inflation rate of over 20 per cent, so, given the scenario, why were appropriate measures not taken?

Moving on to specific events, and shining the torch on episodes documented historically, one sees that after World War I a general assumption prevailed that history would not be repeated. Sooner rather than later, in 1929 a global stock market crash marked the onset of the Great Depression, and economic problems ended the possibility of government resources being available. This led to global deflation and high interest rates, which in real terms meant that what followed was the largest wave of defaults in history until today. It is also a well known fact that once a country slips into default, it may take years and even decades to recover. Given the current economic crisis that prevails today, it may be useful to suggest that in the first instance a better understanding of the problem of debt default is needed in order to design economic policies and crisis prevention, and economic history should have taught us that.

Looking at the underpinnings of any debt crisis, most economists would also agree (see for example, Kindleberger, 2000) that when a country defaults, it is often the result of complex cost–benefit calculus, involving economic, political and psychosocial considerations. For instance, Romanian dictator Nikolae Ceaușescu insisted on repaying, in the span of a few years, the debt of $9 billion owed by his poor nation to foreign banks during the 1980s debt crisis. The readers of this book may remember that on a social and psychological level, Romanians were forced to live through cold winters with little or no heat, factories were forced to operate less due to limited electricity, and unemployment was at uncontrollable levels. It seems therefore that history is littered with such instances, which repeat themselves at various times, thus encompassing all individuals, organizations and societal levels.

Going even further back in documented historical events, one may find that the centrality of *willingness* to repay rather than the *ability* to pay is also a critical issue with regard to economic crises. When one looks back several hundred years to international lending during the sixteenth, seventeenth and eighteenth centuries, it is noticeable that major borrowers were France and Spain, which had armies of their own. History tells us that Britain routinely bullied or even occupied countries that failed to repay foreign debt, and this can be seen in their reason for invading Egypt in 1882 and Istanbul in the beginning of Turkey's 1876 default. Further afield, the US occupation of Haiti in 1915 was rationalized as necessary to collect debt. It is beyond the scope of this book to examine why countries borrow and lend, although a quick assumption is that borrowing money eventually gives other nation states the right to seize assets and to develop strategic relationships.

One may propose that by spending more time in investigating histori-cal events, scientists may find that certain countries may be more vulner-able than others to economic problems and crises – indeed, Argentina (and most of Latin America), in addition to the severe economic crisis it encountered in the early 2000s that all economists and laymen are aware of, appears to have a historical pattern of economic problems and crises. Table 3.1 exemplifies this and clearly shows that certain countries far out-weigh other countries with regard to the frequency of default.

In order to explain the gestalt of such results, Table 3.2 considers exactly the same issue as Table 3.1, but this time in relation to defaulting in Africa and Asia during the twentieth century until 2008. In Table 3.2 the reader is encouraged to note the picture in Asia (and draw some conclusions in rela-tion to issues raised in the previous chapter, where the current economic crisis in Asia was discussed).

With regard to the current economic crisis that is being experienced, Table 3.3, showing the cumulative tally of default and rescheduling, is of particular interest. Once again, it can be seen that certain countries, such as Greece and Spain, have an overwhelming share of years in default since independence. It may be suggested (despite the fact that the authors of this book are not economists) that such information clearly portrays to the outside world that there is an imbalance in terms of *which* countries score higher on such defaults, greatly resembling the current economic crisis and eurozone problems that we are experiencing today. Readers are therefore encouraged to examine countries such as Greece and Spain, which are already highly indebted within the eurozone, with Greece (at the time of writing) having already received its second astronomical financial bailout package, and Spain's government (April, 2012) having just unveiled the most austere budget the country has faced since General Franco's death in 1975, with cuts and tax rises totalling $36 billion (*The Economist*, April, 2012).

Thus whilst each country, each region and each human being is unique, historical parallels can certainly be drawn and history is repeating itself. It can clearly be seen from Tables 3.1 to 3.3 and in Figure 3.1 that in past eras, countries who suffered from great defaults caused unemployment, distress, inflation and taxes rises, on the economic front, and psychological misfortune on the personal level – both of which are strongly interrelated.

The next area to focus on, therefore, is that given the fact that most individuals want the good of society, and most organizations strive for the need for success, why did governments' academics and other profession-als alike fail to take accurate measures to stop this current economic crisis

Table 3.1   Default and rescheduling: Europe and Latin America,
1900–2008

Country, date of Independence*	Years of default and rescheduling			
	1900–1924	1925–1949	1950–1974	1975–2008
EUROPE				
Austria		1938, 1940		
Germany		1932, 1939		
Greece		1932		
Hungary, 1918		1932, 1941		
Poland, 1918		1936, 1940		1981
Romania		1933		1981, 1986
Russia	1918			1991, 1998
Turkey	1915	1931, 1940		1978, 1982
LATIN AMERICA				
Argentina			1951, 1956	1982, 1989, 2001
Bolivia		1931		1980, 1986, 1989
Brazil	1902, 1914	1931, 1937	1961, 1964	1983
Chile		1931	1961, 1963, 1966, 1972	1983
Colombia	1900	1932, 1935		
Costa Rica	1901	1932	1962	1981, 1983, 1984
Dominican Republic		1931		1982, 2005
Ecuador	1906, 1909, 1914	1929		1982, 1999, 2008
El Salvador	1921	1932, 1938		
Guatemala		1933		1986, 1989
Honduras				1981
Mexico	1914	1928		1982
Nicaragua	1911, 1915	1932		1979
Panama, 1903		1932		1983, 1987
Paraguay	1920	1932		1986, 2003
Peru		1931	1969	1976, 1978, 1980, 1984
Uruguay	1915	1933		1983, 1987, 1990, 2003
Venezuela				1983, 1990, 1995, 2004

Table 3.1   (continued)

Notes:
The World War II external debts of the Allied countries to the United States were repaid only by mutual agreement, notably that of the United Kingdom. Technically, this debt forgiveness constitutes a default.
* The years are shown for those countries that became independent during the twentieth century.

Sources: Carmen M. Reinhard and Kenneth S. Rogoff, *This Time is Different: Eight Centuries of Financial Folly.* © 2009 Princeton University Press. Reprinted by permission of Princeton University Press; Standard and Poor's; Purcell and Kaufmann (1993); Reinhart et al. (2003) and sources cited therein.

from occurring? From what has indeed been reviewed we can quite confidently suggest that history is repeating itself, and yet it seems that most logical individuals and organizations would want economic efficiency to be sustainable. A variety of reasons perhaps could be suggested to support the unfolding of negative events that has been experienced in recent years. For example, could it have been that in certain organizations and in certain circumstances people want to serve their own members' interests in the best possible way? So in this case, it may pay to allow for an imbalanced redistribution of wealth to ensue and hence a distributional struggle comes to the forefront (note: readers who wish to understand this issue in more depth are encouraged to read the work of Olson, 1982). Certainly it appears from the worldwide media information that is currently being highlighted that the members of the eurozone countries want to bear the lowest possible share of the costs (whether or not this is ethically correct is beyond the scope of this book). Here one may argue that organizations, countries or regions have a hidden incentive to make their self-interested 'group' in which they operate more prosperous than others, so in essence 'the survival of the fittest' prevails yet again.

A further possible suggestion is that despite all the warning signs being in place and that the 'red lights' were clearly flashing leading up to this economic crisis, most economies failed to take action in due course. By delaying action and cognitively not addressing the issues, the small original problem multiplied like a virus and spread from organization to organization, from bank to bank, and from country to country. Ultimately given such delay, the current economic problems (like other historical problems of the past) have become uncontrollable, the costs of which are yet to be fully addressed and assessed on economical, social and psychological grounds.

The third possibility that may be proposed is that this economic crisis unfolded because of a *combination* of factors rather than as a result of

Table 3.2   Default and rescheduling: Africa and Asia, 1900–2008

Country, date of Independence*	Years of default and rescheduling			
	1900–1924	1925–1949	1950–1974	1975–2008
AFRICA				
Algeria, 1962				1991
Angola, 1975				1985
Central African Republic, 1960				1981, 1983
Cote d'Ivoire, 1960				1983, 2000
Egypt				1984
Kenya, 1963				1994, 2000
Morocco, 1956	1903			1983, 1986
South Africa, 1910				1992, 2001, 2004 1985, 1989, 1993
Zambia, 1964				1983
Zimbabwe, 1965			1965	2000
ASIA				
China	1921	1939		
Japan		1942		
India, 1947			1958, 1969, 1972	
Indonesia, 1949			1966	1998, 2000, 2002
Myanmar, 1948				2002
The Philippines, 1947				1983
Sri Lanka, 1948				1980, 1982

Note: * The years are shown for those countries that became independent during the twentieth century.

Sources: Carmen M. Reinhard and Kenneth S. Rogoff, *This Time is Different: Eight Centuries of Financial Folly.* © 2009 Princeton University Press. Reprinted by permission of Princeton University Press; Standard and Poor's; Purcell and Kaufmann (1993), Reinhart et al. (2003) and sources cited therein.

one issue in isolation. Given the fact that most countries want to serve their own citizens first and bear the least of the financial costs, plus that in a minority of cases certain organizations and individuals want to redistribute the wealth in an uneven and even unfair manner, and combined with a delayed reaction time to the problem, the result has been a potent explosive cocktail. Perhaps in simple terms, or in résumé, others are just

Table 3.3   *The cumulative tally of default and rescheduling: Europe, Latin America, North America and Oceania, year of independence to 2008**

Country	Share of years in default or rescheduling since independence or 1800	Total number of defaults and/or reschedulings
EUROPE		
Austria	17.4	7
Belgium	0.0	0
Denmark	0.0	0
Finland	0.0	0
France	0.0	8
Germany	13.0	8
Greece	50.6	5
Hungary	37.1	7
Italy	3.4	1
The Netherlands	6.3	1
Norway	0.0	0
Poland	32.6	3
Portugal	10.6	6
Romania	23.3	3
Russia	39.1	5
Spain	23.7	13
Sweden	0.0	0
Turkey	15.5	6
United Kingdom	0.0	0
LATIN AMERICA		
Argentina	32.5	7
Bolivia	22.0	5
Brazil	25.4	9
Chile	27.5	9
Colombia	36.2	7
Costa Rica	38.2	9
Dominican Republic	29.0	7
Ecuador	58.2	9
El Savador	26.3	5
Guatemala	34.4	7
Honduras	64.0	3
Mexico	44.6	8
Nicaragua	45.2	6
Panama	27.9	3

Table 3.3   (continued)

Country	Share of years in default or rescheduling since independence or 1800	Total number of defaults and/or reschedulings
Paraguay	23.0	6
Peru	40.3	8
Uruguay	12.8	8
Venezuela	38.4	10
NORTH AMERICA		
Canada	0.0	0
United States	0.0	0
OCEANIA		
Australia	0.0	0
New Zealand	0.0	0

Note: *For countries that became independent prior to 1800, the calculations are for 1800–2008.

Source: Carmen M. Reinhard and Kenneth S. Rogoff, *This Time is Different: Eight Centuries of Financial Folly*. © 2009 Princeton University Press. Reprinted by permission of Princeton University Press.

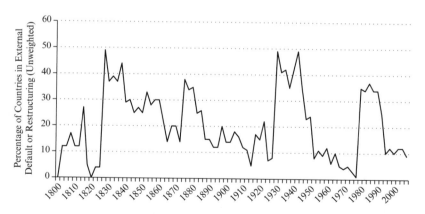

Sources: Carmen M. Reinhard and Kenneth S. Rogoff, *This Time is Different: Eight Centuries of Financial Folly*. © 2009 Princeton University Press. Reprinted by permission of Princeton University Press; Lindert and Morton (1989); Suter (1992); Purcell and Kaufman (1993).

Figure 3.1   *Sovereign external debt: countries in external default or restructuring, unweighted, 1800–2008*

trying to 'save the status quo' or keep monopolies up and running, with compromises and decision making substantially delayed! All in all, such delays prevent rapid adaptation, and thereby reduce the rate of economic growth – which is exactly what is being observed today on a global scale in this current economic crisis.

Furthermore, in learning lessons from the past and in deciding on the future, one should certainly look at other variables which may accelerate or decelerate the success of a nation in economic terms. For example, in the world of work we should explore productivity issues, and monopolies operating in different countries. As early as 1982 Peter Murrell looked at the pattern of exports from the US and various other major trading countries, and found that the pattern of comparative advantage exhibited by the US economy resembles that of Britain more than that of Germany and Japan. This, according to Murrell (1982), and consistent with his hypothesis, is that the United States as well as Britain do relatively badly in older industries and heavy industries that are especially susceptible to oligopolistic collusion and unionization. The author claims that no doubt other factors are also relevant, but the fact that wage rates in the troubled US automobile and steel industries have been very much higher than the average wages in American manufacturing is therefore consistent with and confirms Murrell's early hypothesis. Furthermore, and according to Olson (1982), 'in these troubled industries there have also been excessive numbers of vice-presidents and other corporate bureaucrats with hand-some perquisites'. In concluding this section of lessons learnt from the past, many readers will also remember that in major financial institutions, primarily in the United States, and prior to the beginning of this economic crisis, many CEOs were receiving handsome salaries, almost beyond justification.

One should remember that at the beginning of this chapter the authors referred to a claim that 'after World War I a general *assumption* prevailed that history would not be repeated'. Indeed, if all the warning lights were solidly in place and statistics readily available to interpret, as has been demonstrated above, why then did governments and economic professionals fail to take any precautions before such turbulence began? Why do human beings, therefore, continue to make assumptions that history will not be repeated and negative events will not unfold? It seems that an explanation can only be made based on the psychological factor of 'confirmatory biases'. That is that even perceptions and impressions that we make of people, situations and world economic factors are strongly rooted in psychology. Kassin et al. (2008) questioned, 'why do people fail to revise their opinions often to their own detriment?' It must surely be that we continue to have the tendency to interpret, seek and create information in ways that will verify existing beliefs, commonly referred to as confirmatory biases, and this alone is a strong enough reason to continue to show the willingness only to see what we want to see, to interpret what we want to interpret, and to conclude what we want to conclude. In fact, James Montier, in his book entitled *Behavioural Finance* (2004), suggests to the reader early on that financiers and economists are not rational; rather our insights into irrational minds and markets clearly rest on the foundation of psychology. This encapsulates biases of judgement or perception of reality which is clouded by over-optimism and over-confidence, and can then be applied with the psychological tactics of confirmation bias, conservation bias and cognitive dissonance: in other words, of really only seeing what we want to see.

In concluding this chapter, it can strongly be suggested that given the historical evidence, the knowledge that was available, and the scientific facts that were strongly rooted and evident, the question of whether we have learnt any lessons from the past is clearly answered as NO. We did not learn from the past and the lessons of history did not provide us with a strong enough vision to equip us fully and readily to deal with the economic crisis that unfolded, creating immense stress and anxiety for all citizens involved as well as our financial institutions.

REFERENCES

The Economist (2012). The world this week – only the beginning, 7 April, available at: www.economist.com.

Kassin, S., Fein, S. and Markus, H.R. (2008). *Social Psychology*. 7th edn, Belmont, CA: Wadsworth Cengage Learning.

Kindleberger, C.P. (2000). *Manias, Panics and Crashes: A History of Financial Crises*. New York: John Wiley & Sons.

Lindert, P.H. and Morton, P.J. (1989). How sovereign debt has worked, In *Developing Country Debt and Economic Performance*, Vol. 1, ed. Jeffrey Sachs. Chicago, IL: University of Chicago Press.

Mauldin, J. (2012). All Spain all the time, in *Thoughts from the Frontline*, available at: johnmauldin@2000wave.com.

Montier, J. (2004). *Behavioural Finance: Insights into Irrational Minds and Markets*. Chichester: Wiley Finance.

Murell, P. (1982). The comparative structure of growth in the major developed capitalist nations, *Southern Economic Journal*, 48, 985–95.

Olson, M. (1982). *The Rise and Decline of Nations: Economic Growth, Stagflation, and Social Rigidities*. New Haven, CT: Yale University Press.

Purcell, John F.H. and Kaufman, J.A. (1993). *The Risks of Sovereign Lending: Lessons from History*. New York: Salomon Brothers.

Reinhart, C.M. and Rogoff, K.S. (2009). *This Time is Different: Eight Centuries of Financial Folly*. Princeton, NJ: Princeton University Press.

Reinhart, Carmen M., Rogoff, K.S. and Savastano, M.A. (2003). Debt intolerance, Brookings Papers on Economic Activity, 1 (Spring): 1–74.
Suter, C. (1992). *Debt Cycles in the World-Economy: Foreign Loans, Financial Crises, and Debt Settlements, 1820–1990.* Boulder, CO: Westview.

PART II

Occupational stress in times of a changing world

4. The psychological implications of the economic crisis

In Part I of this book we concluded that historical economic lessons from the past were not learnt. It is in this second part of the book, 'Occupational stress in times of a changing world', that we will assess, in three chapters, how occupational stress in the twenty-first century has impacted on all of us. We are all going through extremely turbulent economic times, which have adversely affected most families, businesses, workers and countries in their ability to survive, and it is exactly these issues that need to be explored. In this chapter we will outline psychological implications of the economic crisis, and in the forthcoming chapters, 5 and 6, we will cover the costs of stress to us personally, both physically and psychologically, as well as the costs for our businesses and countries.

INTRODUCTION

As discussed in the previous three chapters, our current economic crisis is clearly having a tremendous impact on the working environment, as both employees and employers are contending with a host of organizational problems unseen in the recent past. Given these problems, the focal point of this chapter is to obtain a greater understanding of the causes of occupational stress in these turbulent times, and to explore why and how this ongoing economic crisis is impinging on the world of work, creating greater uncertainty and instability for all. It is therefore necessary to now address the world of work, where a host of new occupational stressors have been brought to the surface and which, according to recent statistics, account for a large proportion of workplace sickness and ill-health. Cooper and Dewe (2012) have recently suggested that stress, depression and anxiety currently account for 13.8 million working days lost, or 46 per cent of all reported illnesses, making this the single largest cause of all absences attributable to work-related illness in the UK. It is evident that the occupational challenges that we face due to the salient economic positions of various nations have had far-reaching effects on the world of work. It is acknowledged that each work era features its own unique stressors, but the key today is to address the new work stressors that have emerged and to learn from the past to ensure a more secure and engaged workforce.

Most of the readers of this book will remember how the literature on occupational stress exploded primarily in the 1980s when researchers all over the world focused on the 'demons of the time', which included stressors such as 'relationships with others', 'physical working conditions', the various 'roles' one takes in the organization, and of course, the 'home and work interface' as women began to form an ever-growing percentage of the workforce. Today, admittedly, some of these problems still exist, but at the forefront are other unleashed recession-related problems, primarily issues of uncertainty and insecurity in the workplace. People in many countries (e.g. Greece) are no longer able to meet their daily needs following the collapse of international financial markets, there are mismatched expectations from work and home, and of course the new and severe problem of increased risks of suicide and homicide as people find it difficult to cope. These are but a few critical problems that have emerged in our current times. Today the challenges that we face and the psychological implications of this economic crisis are unique, unseen in the past, and people's stamina to withstand such pressures are only now being examined and put to the test.

These unique problems have led to the most extreme and vicious workplace behaviours seen in recent years, which will be further analysed in the forthcoming chapter. Here, however, it should be noted that not only do we face problems with relationships at work, but this is now seen in the most extreme form of work bullying and violence on an unprecedented and increasing scale (Hershcovis et al., 2007). This should not come as a surprise, however, as in difficult times the 'instinct of survival' takes over, and unhealthy extremes in human attitudes and behaviours take front stage. When one learns of job cuts, redundancies, and well established companies collapsing, despair and anxiety in the workplace are not such surprising emotional reactions. For each individual, such negativities have their own justifiable explanation, but individuals and organizations will struggle to come to terms with these occupational stressors. Indeed each and every person will look at what went wrong and what these consequences mean for them. In addition to having to face and contend with new and fundamental problems at work, we must try and understand the extreme emotional states that stem from these real world events leading to increasing job dissatisfaction at work.

WHY ARE THESE TIMES SO STRESSFUL? THE CHALLENGES OF TODAY

From the moment that the financial crisis erupted in the United States at the end of 2008, turbulence entered the world of work, causing immense changes and challenges to the overall wellbeing of employees, both physical and psychological. During times of economic crises, history has told us that the effects of such crises can become visible and like a cork they can 'float to the top' very suddenly. It is beyond the scope of this book to estimate how fast this can happen, but one may assume that the timing will depend on the overall vulnerability of a particular organization. Certainly with the current economic crisis and financial collapse of 2008, immediate fluctuations in the banking arena and construction businesses were felt (as described in chapters 1 and 2) and it did not take long for governments to restructure their public sectors. Currently, many countries are still in the midst of making firm adjustments to their fiscal policies to align with collapsing economies – Greece being the prime example. In many European countries, such as Greece, Spain and Portugal, economic prosperity was once the norm, and yet once the recession set in, they became the leading countries of economic decline and ruin. This immediately caused detrimental effects in terms of employment rates, and Table 4.1 exemplifies this position by highlighting the recent unemployment levels, which appear to be comparable with levels reached in the US at the height of the Great Depression (Friedman, 2013).

At the forefront, it should be mentioned that an economic crisis causes occupational challenges in a host of domains, as there is a lack of funds readily available to inject into an economy and its businesses. Naturally, this means that there will be fewer people in the workplace, doing more work and feeling more job insecurity. (Table 4.1 depicts a growing and increasing unemployment trend in almost all of the 33 nations reported.) Corresponding to such economic changes, there will be psychological challenges and implications for employees to face as the world of work becomes an uncertain place to be in. Individuals sooner or later will begin to experience such pressures, and will then have a host of questions to address in relation to their confidence in their current jobs and future employment. Questions to be tapped into and pondered over include 'How long will I have a job for?' 'Can I possibly plan for the future?' and within these questions are embedded emotions that occur as a result of our reactions to what is going on – and which clearly seem negative and improper. These emotions may reflect a sense of helplessness and despair, and provoke thoughts such as 'This all seems so unfair and unjust', 'I have always worked so hard and do not deserve such treatment'. Such self-reflecting statements may be translated into work life in the form of

Table 4.1   Unemployment rate: 2000–11 (%)

	2001	2002	2003	2004	2005	2006	2007	2008	2009	2010	2011
EU-27	8.5	8.9	9.0	9.1	9.0	8.2	7.2	7.1	9.0	9.2	9.7
Euro area	8.1	8.4	8.8	9.0	9.1	8.5	7.6	7.6	9.6	10.1	10.2
Belgium	6.6	7.5	8.2	8.4	8.5	8.3	7.5	7.0	7.9	8.3	7.2
Bulgaria	19.5	18.2	13.7	12.1	10.1	9.0	6.9	5.6	6.8	10.2	11.2
Czech R.	8.0	7.3	7.8	8.3	7.9	7.2	5.3	4.4	6.7	7.3	6.7
Denmark	4.5	4.6	5.4	5.5	4.8	3.9	3.8	3.3	6.0	7.4	7.6
Germany	7.6	8.4	9.3	9.6	11.2	10.3	6.7	7.5	7.8	7.1	5.9
Estonia	12.6	10.3	10.0	9.7	7.9	5.9	4.7	5.5	13.6	16.9	12.5
Ireland	3.9	4.5	4.6	4.5	4.4	4.5	4.6	6.3	11.9	13.7	14.4
Greece	10.7	10.3	9.7	10.5	9.9	8.9	8.3	7.7	9.5	12.6	17.7
Spain	10.3	11.1	11.1	10.6	9.2	9.5	8.3	11.3	18.0	20.1	21.7
France	8.3	8.6	9.0	9.3	9.2	9.2	8.4	7.8	9.5	9.7	9.7
Italy	9.1	8.6	8.4	8.0	7.7	6.8	6.1	6.7	7.8	8.4	8.4
Cyprus	3.8	3.6	4.1	4.7	5.3	4.6	4.0	3.6	5.3	6.5	7.8
Latvia	12.9	12.2	10.5	10.4	8.9	6.8	6.0	7.5	17.1	18.7	15.4
Lithuania	16.5	13.5	12.5	11.4	8.3	5.6	4.3	5.8	13.7	17.8	15.4
Luxembourg	1.9	2.6	3.8	5.0	4.6	4.6	4.2	4.9	5.1	4.5	4.8

Hungary	5.7	5.8	5.9	6.1	7.2	7.5	7.4	7.8	10.0	11.2	10.9
Malta	7.6	7.5	7.6	7.4	7.2	7.1	6.4	5.9	7.0	6.8	6.5
Netherlands	2.5	3.1	4.2	5.1	5.3	4.4	3.6	3.1	3.7	4.5	4.4
Austria	3.6	4.2	4.3	4.9	5.2	4.8	4.4	3.8	4.8	4.4	4.2
Poland	18.3	20.0	19.7	19.0	17.8	13.9	9.8	7.1	8.2	9.6	9.7
Portugal	4.1	5.1	6.4	6.7	7.7	7.8	8.1	7.7	9.6	11.0	12.9
Romania	6.8	8.6	7.0	6.1	7.2	7.3	6.4	5.8	6.9	7.3	7.4
Slovenia	6.2	6.3	6.7	6.3	6.5	6.0	4.9	4.4	5.9	7.3	8.2
Slovakia	19.3	18.7	17.6	18.2	16.3	13.4	11.1	9.5	12.0	14.4	13.5
Finland	5.1	9.1	9.0	8.8	8.4	7.7	6.9	6.4	8.2	8.4	7.8
Sweden	5.8	6.0	6.6	7.4	7.7	7.1	6.1	6.2	8.3	8.4	7.5
United Kingdom	5.0	5.1	5.0	4.7	4.8	5.4	5.3	5.6	7.6	7.8	8.0
Croatia	–	14.8	14.2	13.7	12.7	11.2	9.6	8.4	9.1	11.8	13.2
Turkey	–	–	–	–	9.2	8.7	8.8	9.7	12.5	10.7	–
Norway	3.4	3.7	4.2	4.3	4.5	3.4	2.5	2.5	3.1	3.6	3.3
Japan	5.0	5.4	5.3	4.7	4.4	4.1	3.9	4.0	5.1	5.1	4.6
United States	4.8	5.8	6.0	5.5	5.1	4.6	4.6	5.8	9.3	9.6	8.9

Source: Eurostat, September 2012.

Source: Authors' own compilation.

*Figure 4.1   Occupational stress in the twenty-first century: the
              psychological challenges of today*

two competing and contrasting categories as shown in Figure 4.1, denot-
ing that everyday work can be perceived in terms of how the organization
attempts to survive or in relation to how an individual attempts to overcome problems at work. Indeed these two different forces, when opposed,
will undoubtedly create friction.

The two forces in Figure 4.1 may well indeed be contradictory, and
especially so during times of economic upheaval and pressure, as the
organization will attempt to survive financially and the individual (the '*W*'
in our original model in Chapter 2) will attempt to secure his or her own
personal needs and wellbeing.

For the organization, the most natural and immediate response to any
negative and financial outcome is to immediately cut costs and rebalance
the books in the hope that such action will bring about economic improvement. By rationalizing costs and making cutbacks, it is assumed that lost
revenue maybe compensated for. However, in this scenario, action may
also be required which will involve adjustments to the workforce – and
any adjustment involving human manpower will bring about uncertain
psychological challenges which may be painful for all parties involved.
Once the workforce becomes an 'issue under discussion' and 'placed on
the company's agenda', just like other issues, the climate of an organization is likely to change fundamentally. However, in addition to the
organizational climate changing, one must also ask the question of why
these times are perceived to be so stressful for the working sector of the
population. It naturally seems feasible to suggest that today people are
leading their lives around a set of expectations that they have created
about the fundamentals of both work and home, and this is commonly
referred to as the 'psychological contract'. Amongst organizational psychologists, this term is utilized to explain a set of expectations that exist
between us and those around us, all of whom have a say in our sets of
expectations. Certainly, therefore, each one of us has until recently framed

a 'psychological contract' within our world of work, and today our contract of what we expect to obtain at work and what we are indeed receiving is clearly mismatched between the reality of what is on offer in the job domain, and what is actually available for economic survival purposes. In both material terms and psychological terms therefore, it seems that today we are trying to survive the harsh and difficult mismatch between what we have come to expect and what the new uncertain realities at work present us with. For some people, primarily the younger population, this psychological reality seems bleak: evidence shows us (Table 4.2) that youth

Table 4.2   Youth unemployment figures 2009–2011 Q4 (%)

	2009	2010	2011	2011 Q4
EU-27	20.1	21.1	21.4	22.1
Euro area	20.2	20.9	20.8	21.4
Belgium	21.9	22.4	18.7	17.5
Bulgaria	16.2	23.2	26.6	28.2
Czech Republic	16.6	18.3	18.0	18.3
Denmark	11.8	14.0	14.2	14.3
Germany	11.2	9.9	8.6	8.3
Estonia	27.5	32.9	22.3	25.1
Ireland	24.4	27.8	29.4	30.5
Greece	25.7	32.8	44.4	49.3
Spain	37.8	41.6	46.4	48.9
France	23.9	23.6	22.9	22.7
Italy	25.4	27.8	29.1	30.5
Cyprus	13.8	16.7	22.4	26.8
Latvia	33.6	34.5	29.1	27.4
Lithuania	29.2	35.1	32.9	34.3
Luxembourg	16.5	15.8	15.6	16.0
Hungary	26.5	26.6	26.1	26.7
Malta	14.4	13.1	13.7	14.0
Netherlands	7.7	8.7	7.6	8.5
Austria	10.0	8.8	8.3	8.7
Poland	20.6	23.7	25.8	26.9
Portugal	24.8 (e)	27.7 (e)	30.1	34.1
Romania	20.8	22.1	23.7	24.8
Slovenia	13.6	14.7	15.7	16.4
Slovakia	27.3	33.6	33.2	33.8
Finland	21.5	21.4	20.1	19.9
Sweden	25.0	25.2	22.9	22.8
United Kingdom	19.1	19.6	21.1	22.0

Source: Eurostat, September 2012.

unemployment for many countries is at the highest rate ever seen in recent years. Needless to say, for the young, the psychological implication of this current economic crisis is devastating, the costs of which will be assessed in the forthcoming chapters.

The figures in Table 4.2 show that the proportion of young people who are now unemployed due to economic upheaval is incomprehensible, and it seems that full recovery is out of reach and certainly questionable in our current times. Looking closely at the figures, one may notice that for some countries, like Greece and Spain, the percentage of youth unemployment is approaching 50 per cent of the total workforce, and these are young people who are assumed to be both willing and able to secure employment. In the forthcoming chapters, primarily in Chapter 6, the social costs of such trends will be discussed, and light will be shed on the correlation between these figures and social unrest unfolding in many countries, primarily in Europe.

THE CHALLENGE OF WORK CONTROL

For those who remain in the job arena, a host of new problems are emerging as the nature of work itself has undergone a profound transformation in recent years. These revolutionary changes include asking those left in employment to often work excessively long hours to justify the job, and to cover workloads that were clearly carried out by more personnel in the past. In human resource terms, this results in the remaining people often being asked to work well beyond their formal contracted hours. Indeed in December 2011, in the midst of world economic problems, the BBC reported that UK employees are currently working longer hours than most EU neighbours, with an average of 42.7 contracted hours per week but actual hours well above this. Adding to this, Brendan Barber, former General Secretary of the TUC, reported (December 2011) that the figures highlight the extra hours that many people work but which often go unrewarded. Similarly, in a Work Foundation survey (Isles, 2005, cited in Theobald and Cooper, 2012), nearly 40 per cent of respondents said they worked longer hours because they were afraid of losing their job. Thus, it seems that people who are left in employment are faced with a host of problems, including employment rights in terms of hours in the job, their corresponding financial reward structure, and potential zero-hours contracts (where they are employed only when the organization needs them). In addition, the issue of 'control' in the job should now be addressed, and the question to be posed is whether the average employee has a rightful say in the total number of hours being worked on a weekly basis. As early as

1998 Fotinatos-Ventouratos and Cooper clearly demonstrated that there is a fundamental need for all workers, whether white-collar or blue-collar workers, male or female, to feel in control of their job and possess autonomy at work, and this is a necessary requirement for both job satisfaction and overall wellbeing to materialize. Nonetheless, given the current uncertainties prevailing in the economic world, this seems an unrealistic objective to aim for, and one will therefore have to consider at what health costs and organizational costs these challenges are being put to the test. Indeed at the time of writing this book, the eurozone troika of the EC, ECB and IMF are in constant negotiations with the Greek Government and Greek Federation of Workers in an attempt to implement a six-day working week in addition to increasing the compulsory retirement age from 65 to 67. Furthermore, the troika is requesting that employers be allowed to ask staff to work up to 78 hours per week (*Kathimerini*, September 2012). It seems therefore that governmental requests and economic needs are surpassing the health needs of human workforces, at least in Europe. Coupled with this, health specialists need to be cautious about the consequences of implementing such requests, as evidence clearly indicates that working in jobs with excessive overtime is frequently associated with a high injury hazard rate in comparison to working in jobs without overtime (see Dembe et al., 2005).

The challenge of 'worker control' may take another shape and form, as individuals in times of uncertainty may go to extremes in order to 'keep hold of their possessions', and in this case their possession is their job and livelihood. It seems feasible to suggest that people who possess a job will try their utmost to keep hold of it and to gain ultimate control in all domains. Hence, just as one is aware of the instinct of survival, this is the behaviour that now prevails in the working environment: those who can, will attempt to survive – and at all costs. Therefore, in an attempt to secure control in their job, people may go to extremes and be willing to compete and micro-manage others, leading to the scenario of bullying and hostility at work. Furthermore, such individual feelings of uncertainty in the job will certainly spread across the company like a virus, unstoppable. On the other hand, such feelings may lead to positive behaviour – and hopefully greater support and closer bonding amongst colleagues may prevail. Worrisome, however, is when this individual behaviour turns into negative group behaviour, whereby one colleague attempts to gain advantage at the expense of others. It is here, at times of vulnerability, when bullying and hostility may become the emotions prevailing in the company and statistics are clearly indicating that such emotions are on the increase at work (Brough et al., 2009). People willing to gain advantage over others may seek a psychological challenge with their colleagues by attempting to prove their worthiness in the job function over others. One way to conquer this and obtain control is to 'safeguard the job', and here we see the realms of secrecy at work, unwillingness to share information, or alternatively attempting to outpace the others in performance, giving rise to extreme competitiveness in the workplace. By attempting to undermine others, people will go to extremes to outpace the colleague next to them.

In summary, the psychological implications of this economic crisis are that an organizational climate will prevail, comprising psychological stressors such as a climate of suspicion and blame, unhealthy communication, employees wishing to outpace others by working longer in order to gain ultimate control in their working environment and to secure employment during times of economic decline and misfortune.

RESTRUCTURING THE COMPANY AND DOWNSIZING: TWO SIDES TO EACH COIN

As mentioned above, in an uncertain economic world it is natural that each organization will have its own and unique agenda to combat the difficulties faced, and this will include extending working hours for employees, having a reduced workforce, cuts in salaries, and reduced or removed fringe benefits –simply put, overall changes in work contracts and job functions will be subject to severe alterations. Here, however, it is worth noting that the process by which companies may choose to restructure and adjust the workforce is often accompanied by unhelpful language and procedures. For example, terminology such as 'restructuring and aligning the workforce', 'tailoring the workforce to our current economic needs' and 'right-sizing' is used when actually what is meant is job cuts and redundancies. Also, just as the process of informing someone about a job loss is very bad for the person involved, also consider the difficulties that must be faced by the management themselves, who have the responsibility and psychological burden of telling the bad news. From the management perspective, therefore, this is a 'double-edged sword'. For the manager who has to make the announcement of job losses, it is not an easy psychological task, and the issues of concern include, how should management approach the workforce to tell them of the decline in productivity or the loss of income and necessary downsizing of a company? For management who may have been taught in theory of such issues, the reality is now being faced: it should be remembered that during the 1980s and 1990s – the boom economic years – management enjoyed the positive aspects of HR in hiring personnel, and now in the twenty-first century, management has the negative role of firing people. This difficult and challenging scenario has an additional and complicated component – and that is the element of fairness and distribution of justice. But how simple is it to account for fairness, when at work many people become friends, and social interaction is woven into the equation of work relationships and jobs? It is certainly challenging and difficult for management to remain transparent, fair and at the same time carry the burden and psychological implications of job losses to people they have worked alongside for many years. Given this scenario, the way in which the news is conveyed is fundamentally important, and debate exists as to whether it is better to announce job losses abruptly rather than slowly, so that employees are not left in the dark with a great deal of uncertainty. Indeed it has been suggested that waiting can 'accrue its own weight in psychological pressure' (Weinberg and Cooper, 2012) and some sceptics argue that the time itself can offer employees increased opportunity to make life difficult within the organization. However, the European Union and the UK Health and Safety Executive Directives on communicating an impending change in the workforce suggest that the sceptics are out of step (Giga and Cooper, 2003, cited in Weinberg and Cooper, 2012). Levels of anxiety among the workforce inevitably rise as uncertainty occurs, and it is essential therefore that organizations and management pay attention to this, since they are also bound legally to maintain a 'duty of care' for employees' psychological and physical health, through all the stages of the employment process.

Thus far, it could therefore be concluded that the organizational and individual challenges in an uncertain world reflect issues of instability, uncertainty, lack of control, and mismatched expectations from both the organizational and individual perspective (as shown in Figure 4.1), all of which rest on an economic bedrock of fragility and economic erosion. It should also be added here, and certainly not forgotten, that the psychological implications of this economic crisis are also intensified due to the far-reaching effects of globalization. On the one hand, this has meant that the true nature of business on a world scale has incorporated a severe element of competitiveness, and yet, on the other hand, this is resulting in low labour costs unfolding in certain parts of the world. For the worker, however, in all sectors of employment, this means that timescales for production are being reduced, and more worrisome is that given the nature of communication technology the world 'is always on', and there is never anywhere when one time zone or another is not working (Theobald and Cooper, 2012).

THE PSYCHOLOGICAL IMPLICATIONS OF THE ECONOMIC CRISIS: HUMAN WORK MORALE

The above-mentioned troubles lead to a host of other unforeseen problems in the workplace, primarily connected to the theme of work morale and the effects of working relationships, which today are under extreme pressure to function harmoniously and effectively. It is a well-known fact that in past years people sought employment for a host of reasons, including financial rewards and social interaction with others (Fotinatos-Ventouratos and Cooper, 2005), although today, in the midst of unpredictable economic times, the solid foundations where relationships were once enhanced have been eroded, resulting in lack of trust amongst colleagues and a decrease in overall work morale. Early on in the literature, organizational psychologists revealed that the various encounters with people at work can act as both a buffer to stress and also as a key source of stress, as superiors, peers and subordinates can dramatically affect the way we feel at the end of the working day (Fotinatos-Ventouratos and Cooper, 1998; 2005). In recent years, however, due to the ongoing psychological implications of this economic crisis, the pendulum has swung in exactly the opposite direction, whereby we are seeing severe negative effects of relationships with others at work in the form of hostility and violence (Hershcovis et al., 2007). For employees, the accumulative effect of learning that your colleagues have been made redundant seems to be internalized, resulting in the individuals carrying with them a sense of loss and guilt. To that end, in research carried out by Vahtera et al. (2004), it was discovered that during an economic recession in Finland, amongst 22,000 municipal workers, those who in fact retained their jobs following downsizing in local councils reported that the death rate due to cardiovascular disease doubled over the longer term, and increased by five times during the first four years after the job cuts. Furthermore, and worrisome, is the additional problem that management, which is likely to be reduced in recessions, is unlikely to detect or address issues of bullying or reduced work morale prevailing, and professional policies to reprimand negative behaviours are unlikely to exist. Indeed, Jennifer et al. (2003) noted that workplace bullying tends to occur as a result of a combination of negative situational characteristics such as: unfair management practices, organizational uncertainty or change, unsupportive work culture, and job dissatisfaction – all of which seem to be a combination of variables that are evident during economic turmoil. Such findings therefore lead one to conclude that the psychological implications of any economic crisis carry feelings of guilt, anxiety and a strong element of sadness, which can be externalized in a host of ways, thus impacting negatively on overall workplace morale and ultimately the production of employees.

APPRAISING THREATS

As can be seen from the previous paragraph and at various points in this chapter, each person will most likely externalize their problems in a host of different ways, and this is due to the way we perceive stress. For organizational psychologists, it is a well-known fact that if individuals are able to perceive a stressor as a challenge – all the better. However, for some people, this is just not possible and the idea of challenge implies a completely different word: threat. From a psychological perspective, the nature of stress in these difficult times can be perceived in a variety of ways. Doubtless for some individuals and in certain occupations, various challenges may be viewed positively; for example, fund managers and stockbrokers see challenges and uncertainties in a positive way. For others, though, such instabilities are certainly viewed pessimistically, and lead to physical or psychological ill-health and lower productivity. It is these issues that need to be highlighted, since given the economic crisis that is still continuing, many people in the workplace are confronted on a daily basis with economic problems and job threats, as discussed throughout this chapter. Today, the world of work resembles a minefield of occupational stressors, ranging from the possibility of being made redundant, to signing contracts of employment that appear to be meaningless, to facing the negative effects of mergers and acquisitions, and the general feeling of 'what is next', creating an ongoing sense of uncertainty. Furthermore these appraisals give rise not only to a range of negative thoughts, but also to accompanying emotions, which are often revealed in the workplace, for example, through negative behaviours in the form of strikes and work stoppages, bullying, conflict with colleagues, and other negative emotions perhaps leading to feelings of apathy at work. Shedding light on what this means at the organizational level, one certainly can assume that today working people have very different perceptions and attitudes about threats to their job, which will affect their productivity and commitment in the workplace (Warr, 2007). (For a detailed and extensive review, readers are encouraged to view the work of Warr, 1987, 1999, 2007.)

PSYCHOLOGICAL STRAIN

The term 'strain' refers to the negative effects of experiencing high levels of psychological pressure on a frequent basis, such as is being experienced with this ongoing economic crisis. Strain can also suggest a 'cumulative toll' resulting from exposure to daily pressures or the impact of a specific event, for example the prospect of impending job cuts in a workplace, and again this is very likely in times of economic turmoil. This is likely to continue over months, as key decisions are made at higher levels of the organization and hence almost every day is overshadowed by a realm of uncertainty. Further along, and as discussed previously, the stress created by having fewer colleagues may mean that workloads will increase, all of which will take its toll on the individual and possibly spills over from stress to strain. For some, although perhaps the minority, the uncertainties of our times may indeed be viewed as 'eustress', which was first described by Hans Selye in 1956. He believed that many people are suited to situations of risk, but for others situations of risk are only viewed in negative terms, accumulating in strain and, not surprisingly, commonly diagnosed psychological disorders such as anxiety and depression. Indeed, and to be further discussed in Chapter 5, Health and Safety Executive statistics show that in 2006/2007, almost 30 million days were lost because of work-related illness, and furthermore, that stress, depression and anxiety accounted for 13.8 million days lost, making this the single largest cause of all absences attributable to work-related illness (cited in Cooper and Dewe, 2012). In the wake of such data, it comes as no surprise that work-related illnesses seem to be correlated with the economic crisis, whereby issues such as forced cutbacks, presenteeism and decline in job security are increasingly recognized as indicators of psychological strain, which undoubtedly can be reflected in impaired work efficiency in all sectors of the workforce, both in the public and private domains.

ASSESSING OCCUPATIONAL STRESS IN THE TWENTY-FIRST CENTURY

Given the issues that have been discussed throughout this chapter, most readers will conclude that the psychological implications of this economic crisis have certainly created great turbulence in the world of work and across many societies. Such stresses and strains must be put to the test in relation to the psychological costs to our overall wellbeing. Just how fast such stressors will impact on our health is yet to be assessed, and this may depend on the vulnerability of the organization to economic uncertainties, but also on the hardiness and stamina of each person (Cooper et al., 2014). The human being is known to be resilient, and this claim has been stated throughout history, with the early writings of the Ancient Greeks and in particular Hippocrates stating so. Bearing in mind, therefore, that the human being is resilient and is 'put to the test' on numerous occasions, where atrocities can be evaluated and counted over and over again, today we are seeing how the psychological stresses and strains caused by this 'economic war' are resulting in a host of challenges being exposed and confronted at various levels and sectors of human life.

Since the downfall of the financial markets at the end of 2008, the most common thread noticeable in cultures is the unemployment rate, which appears to be soaring on a daily basis. As will be discussed in the forthcoming chapter, the effects of such unemployment hit the individual hard, but the costs and meaning of unemployment go far beyond, with ripple effects for families, friends, neighbourhoods, communities, services and societies as a whole. The meaning of work life, jobs, organizations and employment has created the social strata to which we all belong, and this economic crisis therefore has as its epicentre the world of work and its employees. Not only, therefore, is the human being today being confronted with social problems and natural catastrophes, such as hurricane Sandy in late 2012, but we now have to assess occupational stress in the twenty-first century in terms of other devastating issues, such as redundancies, downsizing, the prevalence of bullying at work, victims of workplace violence and unfair and unjust management practices, all of which rests on the psychological contract which appears to be invalid in our times.

In conclusion, all of these aspects of work life have affected each and every one of us in some shape and form, and the effects of such pressures can only be calculated in terms of losses – losses in psychological wellbeing, physical wellbeing, productivity and morale – the vibrations of which are far-reaching and one may suggest beyond calculable recovery. These issues are evaluated in Chapter 5.

REFERENCES

Brough, P., O'Driscoll, M., Kalliath, T., Cooper, C.L. and Poelmans, S. (2009). *Workplace Psychological Health: Current Research and Practice*. Cheltenham, UK and Northampton, MA, USA: Edward Elgar.

Cooper, C.L. and Dewe, P. (2012). *Well-being and Work: Towards a Balanced Agenda*. Basingstoke: Palgrave Macmillan.

Cooper, C.L., Flint-Taylor, J. and Pearn, M. (2014). *Building Resilience for Success*. Basingstoke: Palgrave Macmillan.

Dembe, A.E., Erickson, J.B., Delbos, R.G. and Banks, S.M. (2005). The impact of overtime and long work hours on occupational injuries and illnesses: New evidence from the Unites States. *Occupational and Environmental Medicine*, 62 (9), 588–97.

Fotinatos-Ventouratos, R.S.J. and Cooper, C.L. (1998). Social class differences and occupational stress. *International Journal of Stress Management*, 5 (4), 211–22.

Fotinatos-Ventouratos, R.S.J. and Cooper, C.L. (2005). The role of gender and social class in work stress. *Journal of Managerial Psychology*, 20 (1), 14–22.

Friedman, G. (2013). Europe in 2013: A Year of Decision. STRATFOR, January, available at: http://www.stratfor.com.

Hershcovis, M., Turner, N., Barling, J., Arnold, A., Dupre, K., Inness, M., Le Blanc, M. and Sivanathan, N. (2007). Predicting workplace aggression: Research reports. *Journal of Applied Psychology*, 92 (1), 228–38.

Jennifer, D., Cowie, H. and Ananiadou, K. (2003). Perceptions and experience of workplace bullying in five different working populations. *Aggressive Behaviour*, 29 (6), 489–96.

Kathimerini (2012). Search for common ground continues, *International Herald Tribune*, English edn, 13 September, available at: www.ekathimerini.com.

Selye, H. (1956). *The Stress of Life*, New York: McGraw-Hill.

Theobald, T. and Cooper, C.L. (2012). *Doing the Right Thing: The Importance of Wellbeing in the Workplace*. Basingstoke: Palgrave Macmillan.

Vahtera, J., Kivimaki, M., Pentti, J., Linn, A., Virtanen, M., Virtanen, P. and Ferrie, J.E. (2004). Organisational downsizing, sickness absence and mortality: 10-town prospective cohort study. *British Medical Journal*, 328 (7439), 555.

Warr, P.B. (1987). *Psychology at Work*, 3rd edn, London: Penguin.

Warr, P.B. (1999). Well-being in the workplace, in D. Kahneman, E. Diener and N. Schwartz (eds) *Well-being: The Foundations of Hedonic Psychology*. New York: Russell Sage.

Warr, P.B. (2007). *Work, Happiness and Unhappiness*, Mahwah, NJ: Erlbaum.

Weinberg, A. and Cooper, C.L. (2012). *Stress in Turbulent Times*. Basingstoke: Palgrave Macmillan.

5. The individual and organizational costs of stress

INTRODUCTION

It was clearly evident from the conclusion of Chapter 4 that the psychological implications of this economic crisis are immense and full recovery is now questionable in the imminent future. From the generic framework that was portrayed in Chapter 4, one can see that given our current times in a changing and turbulent world, the challenges of today are unique, having not been seen in recent years, and following the financial crisis which commenced in 2008, our world economies have collapsed like a falling house of cards. Chapter 4 thus gave a framework for the reader to absorb, from which it should now be crystal clear that the occupational stressors of the twenty-first century are touching the lives of most citizens and organizations around the three major pillars of the global system: Europe, China and the United States. Exactly how severely this evolving economic crisis may be affecting each society is beyond the assessment of the authors of this book; however, what can be asserted is that individuals and organizations are paying dearly, both physically and psychologically, for the new stressors of our times. For example, at the time of writing this book (2013), the rate of youth unemployment in the European Union is gaining momentum, with figures in Portugal, for example, reaching a high of 40 per cent (STRATFOR Global Intelligence, 2013a), the tolls of which will surely be paid both in physical and psychological terms in the near future. Furthermore and more specifically we notice that in certain euro-zone countries, such as Spain, high levels of bankruptcy are undermining economic growth, with Spain's Ministry of Employment and Social Security reporting that a total of 219,000 companies shut down between December 2007 and June 2013, representing a 15.5 per cent decrease in the total number of companies in the country (STRATFOR Global Intelligence, 2013b). And finally, light can be shed on how the crisis has affected young people more than older workers because young people often have fewer qualifications and less experience, and businesses can more easily make this sector of the workforce redundant, especially when they are working under temporary labour contracts. This is exactly the case in the European Union, where between 2008 and 2012 the percentage of young people with temporary employment contracts rose from 40.2 per cent to 42.2 per cent in the EU as a whole, and reached more than 60 per cent within Poland and Spain, which have the highest rates of young workers in temporary contracts (STRATFOR Global Intelligence, 2013a).

It is precisely these factors that one needs to focus on, as today it is anticipated that the organizational, economical and social stressors of the twenty-first century present new realities that the literature has failed to fully address – just exactly because these work and social stressors are new, different and being presented for the first time. In this chapter, therefore, the authors outline these *accumulating* yet rather *unique work stressors* at both the macro and micro levels, whilst an assessment in terms of *costs* at the individual, organization and societal level will be analysed in the forthcoming chapter. Thus, in the final chapter of Part II of this book, the writers will assess the *output symptoms* of stress in terms of the costs of this economic crisis, as once again it is hypothesized that these stressors rest on the pillars of the working population, since ultimately and at the epicentre of our social strata is the world of work, to which we all belong in some shape or form. Given therefore the new stressors of our times, it is necessary to formulate an appropriate model of occupational stress in the twenty-first century and it is anticipated that such a model will be relevant for each of us in the years to come and especially so during this recessionary period. Furthermore, as hypothesized from the beginning of this book, and consistent throughout the chapters, it is assumed that both economic factors and organizational psychological factors should no longer be seen as separate forces; rather these two vitally important spheres are impacting on each other and should therefore be seen as a single entity. In Figure 5.1 the Dynamics of work stress model is presented, which encapsulates in a comprehensive format the macro and micro sources of stress which are predominant in the twenty-first century, with the symptoms of stress at the individual, organizational and societal level being itemized.

MACRO FACTORS

Beginning with the macro factors, our model shows that there are three major forces which are currently dominant, classified as: global competition; global downturn; and government regulation of work. In compact form these can be recognized as:

1. global competition, which is often referred to by economists as 'globalization';

INPUT SOURCES OF STRESS   OUTPUT SYMPTOMS OF STRESS

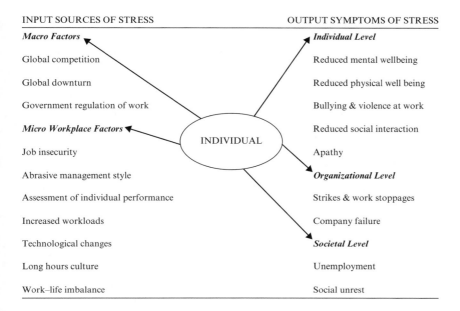

Source: Authors' own compilation.

Figure 5.1   Dynamics of work stress: twenty-first century

2. global downturn, which primarily taps into the eurozone and US deficit;
3. government regulation of work, often viewed in terms of stricter European and US regulations and austerity measures to counteract the above two.

Working with all three input stressor variables, it has already been outlined in Chapter 3 that the effect of this economic crisis is impinging on the world of work and those in it. First, the financial 'crash' of world economic markets and of the US housing markets around 2008 set in motion a variety of economic factors (as outlined in detail in Chapter 3), which sent huge vibrations to other areas and as a consequence it is anticipated that since 2007, the world economy has been hit by the deepest recession since the 1930s (Worrall and Cooper, 2012). Leading at the forefront was the beginning of global competition as different sectors and services all over the world began to compete in a global sector that became restrained in terms of consumer spending. More analytically, the period from 2007 to 2012 has been marked by a radical transition from what economists called NICE (Non-Inflationary Continuous Expansion) to what they now label DRAG (Deficit Reduction Anaemic Growth) (Worrall and Cooper, 2012). From a psychological perspective therefore, one needs to carefully address the effects of such globalization and the heated competition this brings to worldwide trade, as the effects of globalization will surely have an impact on work efficiency and productivity, both of which are strongly influenced by worker motivation and satisfaction. In summary, then, one needs to assess the psychological costs of the transitory period from NICE to DRAG as deterioration in global downturn, and the deterioration in the global business environment reflects worsening market opportunities, increased macroeconomic and political–social risk, and problems in financial systems and ultimately in the psychological aspects of the world of work. Hence, it can first be concluded that the economic global downturn, as highlighted in our model, is a main reason for the deterioration in the international business environment, as average global economic growth is constrained, purchasing power of companies is limited, and as a result, this deep and ongoing economic recession prevails and continues. These factors have therefore created 'high risk' scenarios in terms of both *political and social unrest* (to be assessed in terms of costs, in the forthcoming chapter), and simultaneously in terms of *psychological costs* to individuals and their overall wellbeing. Furthermore, through global downturn, which has seen low growth and an increase in the eurozone and US deficit, there has been a 'knock-on effect' of rising unemployment (for example, currently at a tremendous *total* high of 27 per cent in Greece, and corresponding youth unemployment at a rampant 50 per cent in May 2013). With these problems in hand, governments all over the world, in an attempt to 'protect their own', have been forced to restructure, recreate policies and align with severe and changing regulations at work, which again results in deteriorating relations between governments and increased stress amongst international organizations in all parts of the world. The concluding and visible results are economical, financial, psychological and social.

It is further anticipated that if countries have a worsening overall business environment in the years to come (as a result of slow growth and tightening of government policies), then overall economic improvements will not be possible, and economic growth will continue to be halted, thus creating increased stress in the micro workplace factors listed in Figure 5.1. It should be acknowledged, however, that when applying our model to world economic factors, it is hypothesized that the global downturn has hit hardest in America and Europe, where there is an increase in deficit and low growth, whilst fewer problems have been noticed in Africa and the Middle East, for example. Table 5.1 supports our claim by report-

Table 5.1   *Provision of deficit and debt data from 2009 until 2012*

Euro area (EA-17)		2009	2010	2011	2012
GDP market prices (mp)	(million euro)	8,922,346	9,174,671	9,424,842	9,490,586
Government deficit	(million euro)	−567,420	−569,408	−391,417	−352,683
	(% of GDP)	−6.4	−6.2	−4.2	−3.7
Government expenditure	(% of GDP)	51.2	51.0	49.5	49.9
Government revenue	(% of GDP)	44.9	44.8	45.3	46.2
Government debt	(million euro)	7,136,526	7,831,371	8,225,807	8,600,983
	(% of GDP)	80.0	85.4	87.3	90.6
EU-27		2009	2010	2011	2012
GDP mp	(million euro)	11,754,45	12,278,203	12,647,215	12,902,370
Government deficit	(million euro)	−807,996	−800,889	−561,486	−514,088
	(% of GDP)	−6.9	−6.5	−4.4	−4.0
Government expenditure	(% of GDP)	51.1	50.6	49.1	49.4
Government revenue	(% of GDP)	44.2	44.1	44.7	45.4
Government debt	(million euro)	8,765,652	9,825,306	10,435,932	11,011,797
	(% of GDP)	74.6	80.0	82.5	85.3

Source: Eurostat news release, euro indicators 64/2013, 22 April 2013.

ing the recent and continued euro area deficit, as reported by Eurostat (April, 2013).

According to recent reports by the Economist Intelligence Unit (2009), such macroeconomic environments (as indeed shown in our model) will be affected by increased budget deficits and public debt levels, expected currency volatility and ongoing appreciable risks to asset prices. Therefore, such changes in market forces are resulting in two factors: first, great turmoil is being felt in the *economic and financial worlds*, and second, such changes are taking a heavy toll at the *individual, organizational* and *societal levels* due to the micro workplace factors outlined. Without a doubt, these two input forces are ultimately reflecting on the overall psychosocial wellbeing of all citizens encompassed in this crisis and, taken together, the macro and micro factors result in a time of great intellectual and psychological confusion and uncertainty, whereby the current crisis continues to raise scepticism about market forces and changes in the world of work simultaneously. In summary, it is envisioned that the potential damage to the global business environment and to longer-term economic growth prospects remains high and the costs in terms of occupational stressors and individual wellbeing cannot be underestimated. Indeed the Economist Intelligence Unit (2009) anticipated that: 'The long-standing trend of continually improving global business environments – as a result of robust growth, liberalization and infrastructure improvements – will be halted and even partially reversed in some areas.'

In conclusion, therefore, the macro force stressors have caused the availability of capital to be constrained; to put it simply, globalization is now severely stalled, affecting all realms of the world of work and the people who comprise it. Certainly the idea that the economic crisis will only affect the financial sector and bypass all other areas seems to have proved a long lost myth and illusion. It is without a doubt that this economic crisis cannot be isolated from the social and occupational world and as stated in the title of this book, *The Economic Crisis and Occupational Stress*, these two factors should only be seen as one tight unity where the various forces are working closely together.

MICRO WORKPLACE FACTORS

Job Insecurity

Due to the fact that people are being forced to respond to the economic upheavals of our times, and probably as a consequence of the macro factors stated above, a consistent but strong emerging theme in the world of work is now centred on the issue of job insecurity. It is clear that the world recession has had a profound impact on both workforce attitudes and organizational responses; more specifically, employers have had to make increasingly difficult decisions about their workforce investments and employees are expressing increased anxiety about their future job security. These factors have therefore set the stage for a growing gap between what employees want and expect from the employment relationship, and what employers can afford to deliver in a highly competitive global business climate. One could say, therefore, that the social contract between employer and employee is subject to severe change and certainly people's perceptions of security have changed as a result of the economic decline being experienced. With these problems in hand, the overall impact on the employee in an organization facing an uncertain future is bound to be negative; today it is therefore apparent that people have little influence and 'say' over their work and this is now considered a new stressor of our current times (see Figure 5.1).

Hence, it comes as no surprise to learn that as companies are fighting to meet new demands and therefore trying to survive economically, the average employee at the same time is trying to respond to the work stressors being faced on an almost daily basis. In the early stages of the economic recession (October, 2010), Brendan Barber, then TUC General Secretary, acknowledged that: 'The economic crisis and redundancies have created more anxiety about job security, and as spending cuts begin to bite, and even more jobs start to go, stress at work is bound to increase'.

Indeed and in further support of such claims, Diana Holland (2011), Assistant General Secretary of Unite, told a TUC Disability Conference that: 'This time of cuts and fears about the future is causing tremendous anxiety for working people, and for many workers these are very uncertain times'.

However, research has shown for several years now (see for example, Keita, 2010) that stress on the job can indeed be brought about by organizational change and job insecurity, and therefore puts workers at risk of hypertension, cardiovascular disease and alcohol and substance abuse, and other psychological and behavioural disorders. For example, Siegrist et al. confirmed early on (1990), in a study of 416 middle-aged blue collar workers, that it was the individuals who had been exposed to job insecurity, along with work pressure, who were shown to have a high chance of developing coronary heart disease over a six-year period. Additionally, in other cultures like Korea, research has recently proved (2010) that as a result of the economic crisis and globalization, many workers have been suffering from severe occupational stress due to job insecurity and struggles related to downsizing and restructuring (Min-Woo et al., 2010). Notice should also be taken of more recent and worrisome reports provided by the Towers Watson Global Workforce study (Towers Watson, 2012a), in which 32,000 employees were surveyed worldwide on employee wellbeing and pressure at work. Specifically with regard to the British workforce, the report entitled 'Burnt-out Britain' explains crucial issues, and as stated by Charles Fair, Senior Engagement and Well-being Consultant at Towers Watson: 'This research raises huge concerns over our country's health and well-being at work. Several years of economic uncertainty have led to increased anxiety around job security with workers putting in longer hours than ever, raising concerns of "burn-out" amongst British workers' (Towers Watson, 2012b).

Clearly then, it seems apparent that we are living and working in very dangerous and insecure times, where each day employees are working in an environment saturated with vulnerability and job security issues. Furthermore it seems almost certain that the effects of this financial and economical crisis have completely eroded the time-honoured tradition and belief that jobs may be considered 'for life', with the typical 'company man' and 'solid organization' still existing. In other words these times are now gone and with millions of people all over the world frequently being made redundant, job insecurity is a dominant and worrisome stressor of our current recessionary times. To coincide with such economic changes and challenging working environments, one can see that evidence is showing that the percentage of UK managers working in organizations that were growing declined from 53 per cent in 2007 to 34 per cent in 2012, and the percentage of UK managers who were working in declining organizations had increased noticeably from 19 per cent in 2007 to 34 per cent in 2012 (Worrall and Cooper, 2012). Thus, finally and without a doubt, once job insecurity sets in, other stressors are likely to emerge – almost like a domino effect and to be further discussed below.

INCREASED WORKLOADS GIVEN FEWER PEOPLE EMPLOYED → LEADING TO LONG WORK HOURS CULTURE

As a result of the severe cutbacks taking place in the organizational sector, the remaining people left in the work arena are bound to be faced with increased workloads and tasks that they must perform, creating undue stress and strain. Coupled with this is the ongoing pressure that if employees fail to produce, then there are many people who are willing and waiting to take over; thus job insecurity, coupled with an increased workload from a shortage of staff, certainly creates a strong likelihood of increase in stress being felt in the job. For that reason, and as shown in the Dynamics of work stress model (Figure 5.1), a major source of stress is considered to be the actual amount of work that an individual is currently expected to do, and it is further anticipated that with an increase in economic problems on the one hand, there will be, on the other hand, an increase in workload per employee due to cutbacks and shortages of manpower. Again, as clearly stated recently by global professional services firm Towers Watson (2012a): 'Britain's workforce is heading for a well-being meltdown'. According to the global workforce study previously discussed, it was revealed that more than one in three UK employees (34 per cent) say they are often affected by 'excessive pressure in the job'. Over half (58 per cent) said that they have 'been working more hours than normal' over the last three years, and half expect this to continue for the next three years. Thus it is quite evident from the above citation that not only has the nature of jobs changed dramatically in recent years, but due to the fact that organizations are constrained and that there are fewer people left in the employment arena, this makes the remaining people very vulnerable and forced to work unrealistically long hours and complete unrealistically demanding quantitative tasks. The corresponding costs of such workplace stressors can be further reflected in the continued quote by the Towers Watson study (2012a):

> More than a quarter (26%), have not been using as much holiday or personal time off over the last three years. This coincides with a trend for cutting workforce numbers leaving one in five employees (22%) feeling that the amount of work they are asked to do is unreasonable, with a third (30%), believing the organization is under-resourced.

In a recent statement by Cary Cooper (May 2013), in a study of more than 1,000 working parents commissioned by health care plan provider Medicash, it was revealed that heavy workloads were responsible for increased stress, with more than 60 per cent of respondents saying they found it difficult to switch off from work when at home. Furthermore it seems to be the case that increased workloads are now a severe problem that is deeply embedded in more than one culture, and continued overwork is known to lead to extreme strain. In Japan, for example, there are already words in the language which refer to death from overwork (*karoshi*) and also suicide due to overwork (*karojisatsu*). Furthermore, evidence from occupational stress surveys in other cultures, such as Canada for example, found that: 'Today, nearly 9 in 10 (89%) of Canadian employees say excessive workload is a problem. . .and over the past few years we've seen employers asking employees to work long hours and to do more with less' (Towers Watson, 2011).

Woven into this occupational stressor is the fact that people are now being asked to work unrealistically long hours, simply to cover the workloads that have been set and are expected to be performed, as a result of the effects of globalization, decrease in world trade and the ultimate economic recession. Indeed, this can be reflected in the findings provided by Worrall and Cooper (2012), whereby it was noticed that in 2007 (which corresponds roughly to the onset of the economic crisis), 38 per cent of UK managers worked two hours per day over contract whereas in 2012 (in the midst of the full economic crisis), this had increased to 46 per cent. Thus the average manager worked around 1.5 hours per day over contract to cover workloads, which equates to roughly 46 working days per year. Therefore, as stated previously, a further domino effect and major stressor of our times is now considered to be the long hours culture, which is ultimately of great concern to all.

Long Hours Culture

In 2008, Ronald Burke and Cary Cooper published a book entitled *The Long Work Hours Culture*, in which contributions from experts from six countries addressed important issues such as workaholism, the distinction between passion and addiction to work, and loving one's job! Whilst the overall collection of themes raised in this book is of pivotal importance for all professionals, the gestalt of the results and message conveyed is impressive. Clearly, the stressors of increased workloads and job insecurity (as stated above) are some of the leading and primary factors in contributing to the long work hours culture. However, what should be noted from such findings is the probability that this trend of working excessive hours has emerged due to the possible consequence of globalization and the various embedded macro factors stipulated in the Dynamics of work stress model (Figure 5.1), which has ultimately meant that companies in this time of economic recession have reduced their labour force in order to remain competitive and keep costs down. Indeed, some governments and business leaders have stated early on that employees need to work more hours (e.g. Canada) if their countries are to remain competitive (Burke and Cooper, 2008).

Creating and abiding by the long work hours culture, however, has created a variety of problems for the individual, organization and family unit. First, for the organization, this trend has been allowed to materialize given the current lack of union pressure. That is, several years ago trade unions and work representatives were much stronger and probably would not have 'allowed' such issues to trickle to the forefront as negotiations and discussions concerning working conditions were a fundamental role of the trade unions. It is appropriate here to refer to a personal friend, the late Jimmy Knapp, who as stated in his obituary was 'one of the outstanding trade union figures of his generation' (*The Guardian*, 2001). For readers who are unaware, Jimmy Knapp was the General Secretary of Britain's largest rail union from 1983 until his death in 2001 and was labelled by many in Britain as 'the trade union dinosaur' (BBC, 2001), whereby in holding this position for 17 years he strongly believed and constantly campaigned throughout Britain for all employees and union representatives to be involved in 'full and frank debates, where union membership remain informed and involved' (BBC, 2001). In other words, several years ago employees were acknowledged at all steps of the working process, with decisions being taken on a mutual basis between management and the workforce. Today, however, in this fully blown recessionary period and with weaker trade unions, employees are often excluded from discussions concerning working conditions, thus allowing the long work hours culture to prevail and continue.

Secondly, one must acknowledge that due to the economic recession and turmoil being experienced, companies, both public and private, are working in haste in order to produce and align with the 24/7 on-demand culture. More specifically this means that businesses and assembly lines want to maximize effectiveness by functioning from morning to night, at minimum cost. In addition, other industries, such as the retail industry, are attempting to stay open as long as possible to cater for individuals who themselves are working longer hours in their job. Thus in summary, more organizations today are operating on a 24/7 basis and there is more competitive pressure being put on organizations than ever before, with downsizing and cost containment initiatives being noticeable on an international scale.

Thirdly, in times of economic recession employment contracts are often more short-lived, allowing more excessive workloads and longer working hours to enter the employment contract than previously. Indeed, and as stated in the introduction of this chapter, it is worthwhile to note that currently in some countries, such as Poland and Spain, more than 60 per cent of young employees are working in temporary contracts (STRATFOR Global Intelligence, 2013a), making them an extremely vulnerable group in the total workforce. This is exactly the case of the terrible death (15 August 2013) of Moritz Erhardt, a German student working excessive hours under a temporary work contract for Merrill Lynch, Bank of America, in the City of London. According to information recently released (www.theguardian.com/money/2013/aug/21/bank-intern), this individual was working excessive hours to win a permanent contract and sought-after placement at the bank, which now has put the banks' working culture in the spotlight. Even though this inquiry is still pending, the shocking and shameful conditions of the long work hours culture has led to a plethora of comments and quotes, reproduced in Box 5.1 for readers to absorb. Certainly, and as can be confirmed, the information gathered and provided here leaves all of us in no doubt as to what the micro workplace stressor of the long work hours culture entails.

Finally, it must be acknowledged that the long work hours culture has become problematic for certain members of the current workforce. More specifically, it is a well-known fact that there are more women in the workforce than ever before and given these changing demographics many women have both home and family responsibilities, making working long hours a difficult and problematic issue. For example, early on in the literature, this issue was highlighted in a US survey by Careerbuilder.com (as cited in Burke and Cooper, 2008) who noticed that women clearly reported that they would be willing to take a pay cut if it brought them more time with their children, thus suggesting that some workers would

---

BOX 5.1   BANK OF AMERICA INTERN'S DEATH PUTS
BANKS' WORKING CULTURE IN SPOTLIGHT

'Calls have been made for an overhaul of the long-hours culture among young staff working for banks in the City of London after the death of a "dedicated" German student who had won a sought-after placement at Bank of America Merrill Lynch.'

'A fellow intern at the bank described the aspiring student as a "superstar", adding "He worked very hard and was very focused. We typically work 15 hours a day or more and you would not find a harder worker than him".'

'Chris Roebuck, a visiting professor of leadership at Cass Business School who has held senior HR roles at international banks, told the Financial Times that the overworking of junior employees was an increasing problem in the City.'

'Once a student has come to us, they've already made up their mind they want to work in banking, so the horror stories. . .[don't] put them off'

'Three all-nighters in a row, eight all-nighters: if someone's in single digits for all-nighters, they're one of the lucky ones.'

'It's a glamorous, high octane façade but when you're working it's 12 weeks of 24 hrs. Six and a half days is standard. You will go in at the weekend, you might get a Sunday afternoon off'.

'The spokesperson added that a culture of extreme working hours was mainly restricted to a select number of finance divisions such as mergers and acquisitions but said that "it's even more competitive than it's ever been."'

'They added: "[If] you've got that far, you want to convert from an intern to a full-time role so you will fit in and do what's expected of you."'

Source: 'Bank of America intern's death puts banks' working culture in spotlight', available at: http://www.theguardian.com/money/2013/aug/21/bank-intern-death-working-hours.

---

certainly prefer to work fewer hours and not abide by this long work hours culture.

In summary, therefore, one can see how a vicious circle has developed and unfortunately has been allowed to continue. However, behind this long work hours culture a question must be posed: *why* are *individuals* behaving like this and do people really *voluntarily* want to work such extended hours? Could it be, therefore, that individuals are feeling obliged to comply with and succumb to this new fast demand and extended way of working life? According to a summary of the literature (see for example, Burke and Cooper, 2008), the answer perhaps is both; on the one hand, individuals would rather 'work to live', than 'live to work', although perhaps during this period of economic fragility, where job security is a prominent issue, people feel obliged to work longer than before in order to 'look committed in the eyes of management'. Thus people are arriving earlier at work and staying later than usual in order to show commitment and protect their job. However, such behavioural changes and erratic swings will only probably lead to presenteeism at work. For readers who are unaware of this concept, 'presenteeism' is a term that has been defined by many scientists over recent years, and generally refers to a situation whereby employees come to work despite not feeling well, and therefore perform below par because of that physical or psychological illness. In 2005, Dew et al. described presenteeism as: 'A concept used to describe a phenomenon of working through illness and injury', whilst more analytically, Aronsson et al. (2000) claimed that presenteeism is a concept used to: 'Designate the phenomenon of people, despite complaints and ill health that should prompt rest and absence from work, still turning up at their jobs'.

What one can certainly speculate is that given the micro workplace factors of: long work hours culture; job insecurity; and work overload, these accumulating stressors are very likely to escalate further during times of economic crisis and therefore allow an ideal situation for presenteeism to permeate. Once this sets in, there is a strong likelihood that poor psychosomatic health will prevail, and the costs of working excessive hours will certainly take their toll on family and personal life. Indeed recently (May 2013), in an interview with *HR Magazine* and Cary Cooper, it was stated that: 'A culture of "all work and no play", in the UK is damaging family life, causing high stress levels, cutting time spent with loved ones and creating an inability to switch off from work'.

Further insight on this is given by the recent UK study of more than 1,000 working parents that was commissioned by health care plan provider Medicash, which found that 83 per cent of people felt guilty about the time they spend working and 50 per cent said it had a negative impact on relationships with their children. Nearly half (46 per cent) said it caused problems in their relationships with their partner and caused them to neglect friends (25 per cent) (Cooper, May 2013). Furthermore, and from an organizational perspective, presenteeism is likely to result in increased costs as a consequence of reduced productivity, and according to Goetzel et al. (2004), may be estimated to be four or five times more than costs from absenteeism. In the UK, presenteeism is estimated to cost as much as £15.1 billion annually (Sainsbury Centre for Mental Health, 2007), and as much as $44 billion in the US. Among EU states, the lowest percentages of employees likely to work while sick are found in Poland (22.6 per cent), Italy (23.5 per cent) and Bulgaria (24.7 per cent), whilst the highest percentages of employees who work while sick are in Montenegro (71.7 per cent), Slovenia (59.2 per cent), Sweden (54.7 per cent) and the UK (51.2 per cent), as stated by Eurofound (2010), and cited in Weinberg and Cooper (2012).

Therefore, in summary and with regard to the input stressors discussed so far, one can see that both the individual and organizations alike have jointly contributed to this hectic pace of life that has emerged, and furthermore these workplace stressors have escalated even further due to the worldwide economic crisis being faced. How long this situation will prevail is beyond speculation; however, it can be asserted that these problems will remain for as long as either the individuals or companies are willing to allow the situation to continue, and secondly, for as long as the economic picture remains bleak. Clearly then, our micro workplace factors appear to be 'solidly in place' and resting firmly on the economic macro factors stated. What remains to be discussed and analysed is how technological changes and advancements have also insidiously 'helped' to keep these strong stressors sandwiched together and possibly irreversible in our current times.

TECHNOLOGICAL CHANGES

It is a recognized fact that in recent years technological changes both at work and more generally in society have had an enormous impact on people's lives (Brough et al., 2009) and furthermore these changes have been viewed as both constructive and negative by professionals and laymen alike (Coovert et al., 2005). It is beyond the scope of this chapter to provide a detailed analysis and comprehensive review of all the empirical research which has been conducted in this area, but rather our aim is to highlight to the reader how such technological changes have had an impact on our lives, and especially so during this period of global economic upheaval and turmoil. In this sense, it is hypothesized by the authors that technological changes may have indeed worked negatively and to the detriment of the average employee, and therefore have contributed in creating a further complicated work stressor for an already tired and overloaded employee in this economic recessionary period.

However, one must acknowledge that all technological changes in relation to the working environment have enabled both the worker and job task to 'change' in three possible ways; in terms of increased speed in which a job function is completed; secondly, in terms of how technology has allowed the worker to be 'constantly available', on a non-stop, 24/7 basis; and finally in terms of swift communication emerging. Indeed, in a review of the literature, these three factors are often mentioned (see, for example, Brough et al, 2009). All in all, therefore, one can see that technology is becoming ever more pervasive in the workplace domain, as both workers and the organization per se are relying heavily on this technology to perform their work tasks. For example, this can be seen in the huge growth in the use of PCs, laptops, iPhones, Blackberries, tablets and other various mobile computing devices which have led to increased work flexibility and worker mobility for the individual, as well as enabling organizations to respond more rapidly to immense changes that are occurring as a result of the economic global crisis, within intensely competitive surroundings. However, coupled with these technological changes and to be discussed further on, are enormous dangers and embedded risks in terms of costs to the individual and family unit because of stress, lack of social interaction and respect for private lives, leading to the high probability of ill-health prevailing due to the intensification and overuse of technology. Rather harshly, although perhaps correctly, Albert Einstein stated many years ago: 'I fear the day that technology will surpass our human interaction. . . the world will have a generation of idiots' (Einstein, n.d.). Whilst one may, at first, be suspicious of this strong assertion by Einstein, some may also believe that this day has actually arrived. It is certain that the technological changes that have recently emerged have created a well embedded stress factor that impinges on many people. For example, in an early study by Beaton (2007), it was estimated that workers receive 75 emails per day, but some people may receive as many as 400. To further highlight some of the costs involved, Dennis Kneale, a Managing Editor with *Forbes Magazine*, participated in an experiment as part of a series in which NBC television network challenged people to 'do without' something that had become an important fixture in their life ('Could you do Without?' 2007, cited in Burke and Cooper, 2008). This is a man who started each day with a cup of coffee, two laptops, a cell phone and his Blackberry, and he was challenged to go one week without those pieces of technology. . . he lasted only 40 hours before he tearfully gave up and asked that all his devices be returned.

This example has been mentioned as one may suggest, first and foremost, that technology has acted as a strong aid to the intensification of work in recent years, and it is actually the prevalence of such technology which has allowed the 24/7 culture to emerge, function and continue. Moreover, and more worrisome, is the fact that these technological changes and use of equipment have escalated even more today given the current economic crisis and global downturn. The trend in macroeconomic functioning, which includes downsizing and reorganization to deal with global competition, is resting on the backbone of technology. Hence, it is exactly these technological devices that have ultimately caused workers to become 'overloaded'. As discussed earlier, there is an abundance of evidence which says that current workloads are simply too high for the work to be accomplished – especially in regular working hours – and therefore the individual is compelled to take work home and continue their job outside the normal work-day cycle. Indeed, in a report entitled 'Alleviating employee stress high on employers' "fix" list' (Towers Watson, April 2013), which was conducted in the United Kingdom, it was stated that: 'The majority of employers believe that excessive workload and/or long hours are the most significant causes of stress with some 86 percent citing this as an issue. . . The expanding role of technology – facilitating access outside normal working hours is named as the second highest cause of stress at 76 percent'.

In addition, and to further exemplify the negativities of technology in relation to stress and anxiety in the job, a spokesperson from Towers Watson, in collaboration with the above study, continues. . .

> The trend towards technologies which enable more flexible working have beneficial effects on productivity but also have potential adverse effects on workers as the expectation of responding 'out of hours' rises. . .The combination of working long hours and feeling the need to remain on call outside working hours weighs heavily on some employees' shoulders (Rebekah Haymes, Towers Watson, April 2013).

Hence it is clear and can be concluded that the changing nature of work and demands put upon workers due to globalization have meant that it is technology that has allowed work to encroach in all working time and space. As elegantly and simply stated by Lewis and Humbert (2010), 'Technology has helped us blur the boundaries between work and family life'. The above trends, which began in 2008, continue today, and the pressures on people with increased workloads, the demands in a competitive working environment for the completion of work instantly, and the ability and requirement to interface with people every day in our 24/7 culture, have all been enabled through the technological changes that have evolved.

It should also be remembered, as mentioned throughout this book, that it is during this period of globalization and severe financial cutbacks that technological change has allowed us to 'overload' the worker by reducing the total number of people employed in the labour force in order to be competitive, thereby putting more work on fewer people with the assistance of this technology. As a spillover effect, and as stated in a recent report by STRATFOR Global Intelligence (2013c), it should be noted that Europe's youth unemployment is at unprecedented levels as a result of this economic crisis, whereby in the first quarter of 2013, seven EU members (Ireland, Greece, Spain, Cyprus, Portugal, Italy and Slovakia) had youth unemployment rates above 30 per cent in the 15–24 age range, with Spain and Portugal seeing rates above 50 per cent. Whilst it is recognized that the causes of youth unemployment may vary from one country to another, there are some key common threads, notably that the labour market has become constrained and competitive and that the use of technology is simply adding a huge and additional unwanted burden to these trends, making the global economic downturn (as stipulated in Figure 5.1) and technology appear to go hand in hand.

Therefore one can observe several issues which have arisen from the input of technological change: primarily the current organizational environment and the influence of the global economy have brought about dramatic changes in the world of work and employment trends. All of these changes, trends and organizational restructuring to accompany the effects of globalization have arisen alongside the huge technological advances that we are currently experiencing. In conclusion, however, it is the joint impact of technology and the negative global economy which has had a huge impact on employee stress, psychosomatic health and overall wellbeing in the workplace.

MANAGERIAL STYLE AND ASSESSMENT OF INDIVIDUAL PERFORMANCE

In 1974, Hans Selye advocated that having to live with people is in fact one of the most stressful aspects of our lives. Even though this statement was claimed early on in the stress–strain literature, one can turn this assumption around to focus on the work-group, and it is noteworthy to suggest that good relations with people at work are of pivotal importance – and especially so in the boss–subordinate relationship. Needless to say, research conducted early on in the United States in 2005 by Harvey and colleagues suggested that 13.6 per cent of the working population is affected by abusive supervision (as cited by Donaldson-Feilder et al., 2011). Furthermore, data tell us that there has been an increase in recent years in the number of employment tribunals in the UK; for example, in 2006–07, we saw a cluster of cases amounting to 132,577, reflecting an increase of 17,538 cases on the previous year (Donaldson-Feilder et al., 2011).

Thus one can speculate that as the impact of the world economic crisis becomes greater, it is very likely that healthy and supportive work relations are also being put to the test and tried. Certainly as a consequence of the negative macroeconomic factors prevailing, the workforce has become leaner, and as discussed earlier, the remaining people are expected to work more, which ultimately makes it harder to be supportive and helpful to colleagues at work. Therefore, entered in the Dynamics of work stress model (Figure 5.1) are two critical variables, namely Abrasive managerial style and Increased assessment of individual performance, and it is hypothesized by the authors that how people feel about work colleagues – and most critically, how managers 'manage' – will fluctuate in turbulent economic times. Certainly the current world recession is having an effect on micro workplace factors, and thus maintaining the capacity to manage effectively with limited and perhaps decreasing resources could today become one of the biggest challenges faced by managers.

Indeed, there has been substantial research focusing on the effect of different managerial styles on employee performance and health, with particular evidence being shown by Levinson (1978), who has focused on the impact of the 'abrasive manager', who is characterized as: 'Achievement oriented, hard-driving and intelligent, but function[s] less well at the emotional level' (cited in Hurrel Jr et al., 2011).

It is, however, very unfortunate that according to such research (Hurrel Jr et al., 2011), it is exactly this abrasive managerial style that appears to be the dominant leadership pattern during recessionary and downturn periods. This is probably so since in difficult economic times an abrasive management style is likely to emerge as the pressure accumulates on managers and employees to justify their jobs and simultaneously to meet their performance and target levels in all sectors of employment. It is therefore perhaps obvious that extreme or abrasive management styles and increased assessments of individual performance can lead to psychological distress and have a significant impact on the health of employees. More recently, for example, in the UK Government Foresight Project on Mental Capital and Wellbeing (Government Office for Science, 2008), it was clearly highlighted that managerial style is implicated in people's health and wellbeing at work. This suggests that, more than ever, managers should be equipped with the necessary skills, knowledge and capacity to manage their workforce effectively, especially in turbulent economic times.

In returning, therefore, to the title of this book, *The Economic Crisis and Occupational Stress*, it can now be clearly seen how the pieces of the jigsaw puzzle are slowly coming together to form a coherent whole. In the context, therefore, of managerial styles and increased assessments of individual performance, one can see that in times of economic difficulty the effects of financial problems are far-reaching and can be felt in the organization itself and at different managerial levels. Indeed, this was nicely summed up by Sir Paul Judge (Chairman of the Academic Advisory Council Chartered Management Institute, 2013) recently, who stated:

> The way that people in positions of authority exercise leadership and management has a decisive influence on performance of their own organisation and therefore of the wider economy. . . An important conclusion is that some senior

managers who drive down costs are damaging wellbeing and thereby contributing to long term false economies.

To reinforce the above statement, we need to look at where we currently are in this prolonged economic downturn by reflecting on the past and therefore providing a vision for the future. This is precisely what was done in groundbreaking research by Les Worrall and Cary Cooper who surveyed a cohort of 10,000 managers at all levels in the United Kingdom from 2007 to 2012. In their research Worrall and Cooper examined the interface at the period before the recession (2007) and again in 2012, and then viewed the impact on numerous variables, such as hours, job insecurity, workload, and changes in management style. Of particular evidence in this economic period is that: 'We now have a much more abrasive bureaucratic and autocratic management style as a result of this recession' (as quoted by C.L. Cooper, at Management Article of the Year Award, Chartered Management Institute, January 2013).

There is therefore strong evidence that this cycle of economic decline is compounded by damaging leadership styles and uninspiring management behaviour, and this has occurred despite the fact that it has been proven in the past (Worrell et al., 2011) that there is a strong relationship between the quality of a worker's relationship with their line manager and their level of employee engagement, job satisfaction and sense of empowerment. These findings, furthermore, are not only applicable in cultures such as the United Kingdom, but are also found as far away as China, where in recent research conducted by Alex Ning Li and Hwee Hoon Tan (2013) in an article entitled 'What happens when you trust your supervisor?' it was clearly found that trust in one's supervisor contributes to improved job performance.

It seems therefore, without a fraction of doubt, that today in the midst of economic poverty the spillover effects in terms of management style and increased assessment of individual performance have progressively worsened since 2007. This, coupled with the prevailing euro crisis, austerity and rising commodity prices, has made life very challenging for all of us, leading to a deterioration of several indicators, including negative management styles and more frequent scrutiny of individuals in their jobs, which surely depress employment wellbeing and productivity.

WORK–LIFE IMBALANCE

Give parents at work a passport to help them work more flexibly (Cary Cooper, 9 January, 2013)

As more couples today are two-income families, and most likely working long hours, it comes as no surprise to learn (Antoniou and Cooper, 2013) that the demands put upon people in these turbulent economic times are ultimately taking their toll on their working and private lives. Given the accumulating stressors that have been mentioned throughout this chapter, ranging from work overload, to the extreme use (or abuse) of technology and the long work hours culture, the resulting factor is clearly a costly change in the divide between work and home. In other words, the 'boundaries' that were once solidly in place, with the popular '9.00 am – 5.00 pm' routine being acknowledged and adhered to, have been eroded in order to counteract the negativities that have occurred from the worldwide recession. Entering approximately the sixth year of global economic crisis, it is now clear that the entire nature of work has dramatically changed, and with fewer people doing even more work, the issues of a respectful work–life balance and reasonable working hours are now part of a past era of prosperity. This trend has occurred despite the vast amount of literature (see for example Brough and O'Driscoll, 2005) that has documented the psychological impact of stressors at the home and work interface, with well-recognized effects such as depression and increased alcohol consumption occurring when the work–life balance is severely disrupted (Noor, 2002).

This is so much so, that the literature over recent years has attempted to provide suitable definitions to accurately reflect and portray the meaning of work–life balance, with Kalliath and Brough's (2008) definition being well acknowledged: 'Work–life balance is the individual perception that the work and non work activities are compatible and promote growth in accordance with an individual's current life practices'.

Yet the problem is more severe today, as it should be recognized that this particular work stressor is not an isolated problem to be found in only a few countries and cultures, but rather its negative effects are being felt in most corners of the globe, and they are most likely increasing due to significant reorganization or downsizing of firms to counteract the global recession. For example, the most recent studies conducted by Towers Watson (2012) in various cultures shed light on this. In their latest (2012) Health, Wellbeing and Productivity survey, it is revealed that: 'Almost all (98%) of employers. . . feel that stress is an issue for their workforce, whilst a similar percentage (97%) believe work–life balance is also an issue' (Rebekah Haymes, Senior Consultant at Towers Watson, 2013).

Similarly, in other cultures, namely in the Asia Pacific, where more than 9000 employees were polled in 2012, it was revealed that stress, work–life balance and workload are collectively identified as the most important driver for sustainable engagement; however, workers are struggling to cope in this aspect. In addition, in this latter survey it was also noticed that there is a growing trend for employees in the Asia Pacific region (specifically, including the fast-growing economies such as China, India, Indonesia, Malaysia and the Philippines) to use fewer paid time-off days than in the past. Also, perhaps even more worrisome is the fact that when employees in the Asia Pacific were asked to provide a vision for the future, it was stated that more than half of them also expect to work more hours than normal in the next three years to come!

One may therefore argue that the healthy relationship between home and work life is dramatically changing on an international scale and this is certainly not surprising given the huge drop in job security that is prevailing in most societies, correlating with the global downturn. Furthermore and coupled with the fact that today there is a noticeable increase in the amount of presenteeism evident in organizations, the end result is surely potential damage to home and work balance, with adverse effects on relationships with partners and/or children. Early in 2000, in their study Linehan and Walsh interviewed female senior managers who revealed that women experienced extra strain and guilt feelings about balancing an international career with family responsibilities.

Moreover, in an attempt to survive these modern day stressors, one is also noticing a changing trend in childrearing practices, through either paid alternatives or relying on family networks to assist, which is certainly the trend in continental Europe – Greece, for example. However, whilst these are immediate solutions for dual career couples, there is still a great necessity for good and adequate child care provisions to be available, with substitutes of all kinds taking second place to parental supervision and care. However, an additional worrisome scenario that has emerged is the fact that as a result of cutbacks and shortages taking place in most European countries, we learn of essential facilities that families have relied on in the past, such as local council funded nursery schools and day care centres, being closed by the local governments in order to reduce public spending. Such initiatives may indeed be reducing public spending, although once again the cost of such government initiatives is being paid for by families themselves who are now in a serious financial dilemma of where to leave their children in order to work. One may suggest, therefore, that if this is the case, and indeed 'no light seems to be emerging at the end of the tunnel', then perhaps suitable suggestions for coping with new work–life imbalances need to be addressed and implemented in order to coincide with the demanding macroeconomic factors prevailing. Indeed earlier on in the year, the introductory quote made by Cary Cooper implies that alternative working arrangements that offer employees flexibility – such as part-time work, job sharing and working from home, may be feasible solutions to investigate during recessionary and high demand work periods. Furthermore, and given this upcoming severe workplace stressor, notice should be taken of legal issues, such as the UK Employment Act (2002), which supports the right of employees with responsibilities to care for children and elders to request flexible working arrangements from their employer (Weinberg and Cooper, 2007). What is certainly the case, and which is to be discussed further in this book, is the fact that work–life imbalance is a fully emerged stressor of our times, and suitable solutions need to be addressed in a simultaneous triangular format – namely, at the individual, organizational and certainly societal level.

SUMMARY

Having discussed some of the major input work stressors that we believe exist during this time of economic turbulence and fragility, we are now in a position to certify to the reader how *both* the macroeconomic factors and the micro workplace factors have ruthlessly and negatively combined together to formulate an equation of *The Economic Crisis and Occupational Stress*, as stated in the title of this book. Secondly, the reader, whether they be academic, researcher, student or layman, should now fully understand how this equation is currently unfolding to produce unwanted consequences for all people, families and organizations encapsulated in this economic collapse and huge global downturn. What remains the case, however, is to assess how this economic crisis, with its fragmented landscape and given occupational stressors, will have an effect on the behaviour, psychological functioning and overall wellbeing in the years to come – and this needs to be examined at three levels: the individual level, organizational level and societal level.

CONCLUSION

In this chapter the authors have outlined to the reader how the world of work is currently undergoing a profound transformation, with the 'direction of the waves' still to be determined as work continues to be filled with turbulence and uncertainty. This transformation is unique and has not been seen in recent years, thus making employment a vulnerable domain for the average person in most societies during this ongoing recessionary period. Whilst it is acknowledged that most people seek work for a variety of reasons – financial reasons usually being the primary motivator – it should be remembered that work satisfies many inborn psychological needs that the human being possesses, for example social needs, recognition needs, creative needs and belonging needs. Yet today these needs are hardly touched upon, as the worker is divided by the satisfaction that work should offer us, as opposed to what the world of work is, in reality, presenting us with. The fact is that our world of work is heavily influenced and 'contaminated' with extraneous variables dominated by the world economy and the position that globalization and world affairs is creating. Such market forces and macroeconomic factors that once were present, although rather peripherally addressed in relation to psychology and the world of work, are today the driving forces underlying the employment arena. Thus previous models in relation to occupational stress put forward by organizational psychologists and scientists alike are perhaps not so relevant during this world economic crisis, as other key issues are at the forefront that urgently need to be addressed. Hence, however one may view the psychology of industry, the variables encapsulated in the stress–strain arena have been clearly hypothesized by the authors, and furthermore discussed in relation to the Dynamics of work stress model outlined throughout this chapter, and it is believed such a model needs to be referred to by academics and practitioners alike in the forthcoming years. In conclusion, therefore, it is strongly believed that the input stressors of work psychology contain two elements, namely the macro and micro factors, which are insidiously combined to form a coherent whole. What now remain to be assessed in the forthcoming and final chapter of Part II of this book are the costs of such stressors in terms of mental, physical and social status to provide a complete reference and guide for wellbeing and health at work.

REFERENCES

Antoniou, A.S. and Cooper, C.L. (2013). *The Psychology of the Recession on the Workplace*. Cheltenham, UK and Northampton, MA, USA: Edward Elgar.

Aronsson, G., Gustafsson, K. and Dallner, M. (2000). Sick but yet at work: An empirical study of sickness presenteeism. *Journal of Epidemiology and Community Health*, 54, 502–9.

Barber, Brendan (2010). Stress tops workers' safety concerns and spending cuts will make it worse. 28 October, UK National Work-Stress Network, available at: http://www.workstress.net.

BBC (2001). Jimmy Knapp: Old school, new ideas, 13 August, BBC News, available at: news.bbc.co.uk/1/hi/scotland/1499579.stm.

Beaton, E. (2007). Work is driving me crazy. *Atlantic Business*, 18 (4), 36–45.

Brough, P. and O'Driscoll, M. (2005). Work–family conflict and stress, in A. Antoniou and C. Cooper (eds), *A Research Companion to Organizational Health Psychology*, Cheltenham, UK and Northampton, MA, USA: Edward Elgar, pp. 346–65.

Brough, P., O'Driscoll, M., Kalliath, T., Cooper, C.L. and Poelmans, S.A.Y. (2009). *Workplace Psychological Health: Current Research and Practice.* Cheltenham, UK and Northampton, MA, USA: Edward Elgar.

Burke, R.J. and Cooper, C.L. (2008). *The Long Work Hours Culture: Causes, Consequences and Choices.* Bingley: Emerald Group Publishing Limited.

Cooper, C.L. (May 2013). 'UK has a cultural problem of "overworking"', says HR thinker Cary Cooper, *HR Magazine*, 16 May, available at: http://www.hrmagazine.co.uk/hro/news/1077237/uk-cultural-overworking-hr-thinker-cary.

Cooper, C.L. (2013). Speech at Management Article of the Year Award, available at: www.theguardian.com/uk.

Coovert, M.D., Thompson, L.F. and Craiger, J.P. (2005). Technology, in J. Barling, E.K. Kelloway and M.R. Frone (eds), *Handbook of Work Stress.* Thousand Oaks, CA: Sage Publications, pp. 299–324.

Dew, K., Keefe, V. and Small, K. (2005). Choosing to work when sick: Workplace presenteeism. *Social Science & Medicine*, 60, 2273–82.

Donaldson-Feilder, Emma, Yarker, Joanna and Lewis, Rachel (2011). *Preventing Stress in Organizations: How to Develop Positive Managers.* Chichester: John Wiley.

Economist Intelligence Unit (May 2009). Globalisation stalled: How global economic upheaval will hit the business environment. Special Report, London: Economist Intelligence Unit.

Einstein, Albert (n.d.). I Fear the Day that Technology Will Surpass Human Interaction, available at: http://quoteinvestigator.com /2013/03/19/tech-surpass.

Goetzel, R., Long, S., Ozminkowski, R., Hawkins, K., Wang, S. and Lynch, W. (2004). Health, absence, disability and presenteeism cost estimates of certain physical and mental health conditions affecting US employers. *Journal of Occupational and Environmental Medicine*, 46, 398–412.

Government Office for Science (2008). Mental capital and wellbeing: Making the most of ourselves in the 21st century. UK Government Foresight Project, London: The Government Office for Science.

The Guardian (2001). Rail union leader Jimmy Knapp dies. 14 August, *The Guardian*, available at: www.theguardian.com/politics/2001/aug/14/uk.politicalnews.

Holland, Diana (2011). Unite takes on stress epidemic, taken from TUC Risks 507, 28 May, UK National Work-Stress Network, available at: http://www.workstress.net.

Hurrel, Jr, Joseph J., Levi, Lennart, Murphy, Lawrence R. and Sauter, Steven L. (eds) (2011). *Encyclopedia of Occupational Health and Safety*, Jeanne Mager Stellman, Editor-in-Chief. Geneva: International Labor Organization.

Judge, Sir Paul (2013). Chartered Management Institute *Management Articles of the Year*, CMI: London.

Kalliath, T. and Brough, P. (2008). Work–life balance: A review of the meaning of the balance construct. *Journal of Management and Organization*, 14 (3), 323–7.

Keita, Gwendolyn Puryear (2010). Calling more attention to worker stress. *Monitor on Psychology*, 41 (4), 56, available at: http://www.apa.org/2010/04/itpi.aspx.

Levinson, H. (1978). Problems that worry executives. In A.J. Marrow (ed.), *The Failure of Success.* New York: AMACON.

Lewis, S. and Humbert, A.L. (2010). Discourse or reality: 'Work–Life Balance' flexibility and gendered organizations. *Equality Diversion and Inclusion*, 29 (3), 239–54.

Linehan, M. and Walsh, J.S. (2000). Work–family conflict and the senior female international manager. *British Journal of Management*, 11, S49–S58.

Min-Woo, Jong, Ho Chae, Jeong and Chan Choi, Soo (2010). Crisis intervention for workers in severely stressful situations after massive layoffs and labor disputes. *Journal of Preventive Medicine and Public Health*, 43 (3), 265–73.

Ning Li, A. and Hwee Hoon Tan (2013). What happens when you trust your supervisor? Mediators of individual performance in trust relationships. *Journal of Organizational Behaviour*, 3, 407–25.

Noor, N.M. (2002). Work–family conflict, locus of control and woman's well-being: Test of alternative pathways. *Journal of Social Psychology*, 142 (5), 645–62.

Sainsbury Centre for Mental Health (2007). Mental health at work: Developing the business case. Policy Paper No. 8. London: Sainsbury Centre for Mental Health.

Selye, H. (1974). *Stress without Distress*. Philadelphia: Lippincott.

Siegrist, J., Peter, R., Junge, A., Cremer, P. and Seidel, D. (1990). Low status control, high effort at work and ischaemic heart disease: Prospective evidence from blue collar men. *Social Science and Medicine*, 31, 1127–34.

STRATFOR (2013a). Youth unemployment in the European Union, 29 May, STRATFOR Global Intelligence, available at: www.stratfor.com.

STRATFOR (2013b). In Spain, bankruptcies undermine economic growth, 8 August, STRATFOR Global Intelligence, available at: www.stratfor.com.

STRATFOR (2013c). Greek's radical left: The dangers of the disaffected and the unemployed, 14 March, STRATFOR Global Intelligence, available at: www. stratfor.com.

Towers Watson (2011). Investing in workforce health generates higher productivity. Workplace stress is at crisis levels, Toronto, 21 November, available at: http://www.towerswatson.com/en/Press/2011/11.

Towers Watson (2012a). 2012 Global Workforce study, available at: http://www. towerswatson.com/global-workforce-study/reports.

Towers Watson (2012b). Burnt-out Britain: One-in-three employees face excessive pressure at work, available at: http://www.towerswatson.com/en/Press/2012/11.

Towers Watson (2013). Alleviating employee stress high on employers' 'fix' list, United Kingdom, 23 April, available at: http://www.towerswatson.com/en/ Press/2013/04.

Weinberg, A. and Cooper, C.L. (2007). *Surviving the Workplace: A Guide to Emotional Well-being at Work*. London: Thomson Learning.

Weinberg, A. and Cooper, C.L. (2012). *Stress in Turbulent Times*. Basingstoke: Palgrave Macmillan.

Worrall, L. and Cooper, C.L. (2012). *The Quality of Working Life 2012: Managers' Wellbeing, Motivation and Productivity*. London: Chartered Management Institute (CMI).

Worrell, L., Cooper, C.L. and Lindorff, M. (2011). A picture of trust in UK business organizations. In Searle, R. and Skinner, D. (eds), *Trust and Human Resource Management*. Cheltenham, UK and Northampton, MA, USA: Edward Elgar

6. The consequences of occupational stress in times of a changing economic world

INTRODUCTION

In the previous chapter, we outlined to the reader the various macro and micro occupational stressors that have emerged during this ongoing recessionary period, and furthermore these stressors have been discussed in relation to the Dynamics of work stress model presented in the previous chapter (Figure 5.1). Whilst certain countries are indeed showing the first signs of financial recovery from the worst economic crisis experienced since the Great Depression of the 1930s, it is also understood that the position of economic affairs needs to be assessed globally and not looked at in relation to one or two specific countries in isolation. This is necessary as the economic status of one country will certainly cause friction and turmoil in neighbouring countries, and such is the case that the effects of globalization and corresponding negative world affairs are seen to be interdependent, thereby affecting all employees in most societies at the current time. Furthermore the economic problems today are unlike previous world economic problems of the past and, more specifically, it should be acknowledged that the current world economic crisis is a crisis of 'debt' and not a crisis of 'demand'. Whilst the authors of this book are not economists, it is understood that most societies and governments appear to be lacking the appropriate funds to inject back into the economy, or even if financial reserves are available, most financial sectors and banks are highly reluctant to lend money and allow for borrowing to occur. This is of particular concern to organizational psychologists, as it is suggested that until financial reservoirs are opened up, employment and the corresponding world of work will continue to be severely affected. For example, reports have emerged (October 2013) that unemployment in economically troubled Greece is anticipated to remain at a tremendous high of 34 per cent until the year 2016 (Eurostat, 2013). As shown in the previous two chapters, employees and organizations remain highly vulnerable, and any minor fluctuation in economic and financial affairs will certainly have consequences in terms of stress and strain emerging both at work and at home in this changing world. The consequences of such stressors in relation to employees, organizations and most societies at stake are now examined and Box 6.1 provides a few examples of current world economic affairs and their corresponding negative consequences in terms of overall wellbeing, both within and outside the work domain.

THE COSTS OF STRAIN AT THE INDIVIDUAL LEVEL

It can be seen that the consequences of macro- and microeconomic and financial movements will certainly be strongly felt by most employees and companies and any slight economic and financial improvement in one country certainly does not justify the assumption that the 'global recovery' is about to take place. More worrisome for organizational and social psychologists is the fact that in the near future the economy may indeed begin to improve; however, this does not automatically mean that the next day will also be more effective for citizens and workers. Thus we may be 'lucky', and eventually the economic crisis may begin to fade; however, the psychological consequences of this world crisis will still remain for a very long time and employees are likely to still feel insecure, affected and damaged. Whilst human beings are resilient and able to change, how quickly and how successfully they are able to adapt to these global macro-economic changes is not known. It could be speculated that it may take decades for our physiological and psychological characteristics to adapt to our changing and demanding environment, and yet these huge changes that we have been confronted with, both at home and at work, have demanded considerable immediate adaptations.

Considering the consequences of such worldwide economic problems, the output symptoms of strain at the individual level can be examined. Table 6.1 indicates immediately to the reader how physical and psychological symptoms have indeed increased in managerial occupations, coinciding with the accurate timing of the prevailing economic crisis (Worrall and Cooper, 2012).

As seen from Table 6.1, the effects of the worldwide crisis can be observed in this cohort of 10,000 UK managers from shop floor to top floor, with high percentages being reported in terms of workers suffering from extreme tiredness (61 per cent), sleep loss (60 per cent) as well as muscular tension/aches and pains (57 per cent). Certainly then the impact has had profound effects on both the psychological and physical health of people in the private and public sector. Indeed, epidemiologists have

BOX 6.1   CITATIONS OF RECENT GLOBAL AFFAIRS

'The end of the welfare state in Europe' (STRATFOR, 18 September 2013):
   'In a televised speech before the Dutch parliament on Tuesday, King Willem-Alexander said that the welfare state of the 20th Century is gone and should be replaced by a society in which people create their own social and financial nets with less help from the state. The focus of the address, written for the king by the Prime Minister Mark Rutte's Government, was that the current levels at which the state pays for unemployment benefits and subsidized health care are unsustainable amid Europe's ongoing woes'.

'Care homes see mass exodus: thousands of Greek families opting to take family members out of nursing facilities' (*International Herald Tribune*, Greek edn *Kathimerini*, 18 September 2013):
   'Grandma and grandpa's pension has become the main source of income for thousands of Greek families struggling with unemployment, along with rising living costs and taxes. This shift has been accompanied by a mass evacuation of retirement homes across the country as elderly family members move in with their children and grandchildren in order to make ends meet'. . ..'Most of the unemployed people in this country are surviving on the pensions of their parents and grandparents'. . ..and 'How the situation develops depends entirely on the course of the Greek economy'.

'In Germany, Merkel will seek a new coalition' (STRATFOR, 23 September 2013):
   'Despite the European Crisis and slowing German economy, Merkel's Christian Democratic Union and the Christian Social Union managed to gain more seats in the parliament than during the 2009 elections'. . ..'For the past four years, Berlin has managed to maneuver Germany out of the global financial crisis and through the European crisis with minimal damage. The next four years are likely to be more challenging because of the scope of the European Crisis; the effects of Europe's unemployment crisis have yet to be felt'.

'Suicide rates increased by 45 per cent' (APA PsycPort, 10 September 2013):
   '"Suicides increased by 45 per cent during the first four years of Greece's financial crisis", a mental health aid group said, warning there are indications of a "very large rise".'

'Bank of America intern's death put banks' working culture in spotlight' (*The Guardian*, 21 August 2013):
   'For reasons related to an individual's ambition or the current employment market, people are pretty desperate to get jobs'.

'Third Quarter Forecast 2013' (STRATFOR, 9 July 2013):
   'The sovereign debt crisis was just the first phase of a much deeper socioeconomic predicament'. . ..'The larger crisis will take time to play out, but it will tear at the foundation of the European Union. Indeed, unemployment rates will continue to climb and increasingly affect the core of Europe'. . ..'France's unavoidable task

of trying to improve the competitiveness of its economy will take the form of debate over pension reform and the sensitivity of the issue will likely lead to street protests by some labor unions in France'.
'Third Quarter Forecast 2013' (STRATFOR, 9 July 2013):
   'China's financial instability will remain a central preoccupation. . .With massive debt, hidden risks, slowing growth and a new administration seeking to establish credibility, the conditions exist for more banks and companies to default, aggravating the situation. The general slowdown will force China's leadership to contend with layoffs, bankruptcies, protests and trade frictions with the developed world'.

'EU: Car sales drop to lowest recorded level' (Bloomberg, 17 September 2013):
   'Car sales in Europe dropped in August, reducing deliveries to their lowest level since records started in 1990'. . .'Registrations fell 4.9 per cent from the previous year, and eight-month sales dropped 5.2 per cent'.

'Are economic stagnation and unemployment fueling social unrest?' (International Labour Organization, 8 July 2013):
   'From Tahrir Square to Wall Street, growing economic inequalities and a persistent lack of jobs have caused demonstrators in many countries to demand real change from their governments. But as the global economy recovery stalls and high unemployment rates persist, the root causes of social unrest show no signs of abating'.

shown in the past that there is a strong connection between human health and the work environment, although health professionals acknowledge that there is often a time lag between the experience of stress and the onset of medical symptoms and ill-health (Theorell, 2011). What is certain from the literature available is that illness and disease are often stress-related, and they appear to have intensified under poor economic and financial conditions. Early on in the literature many effects of occupational stress were acknowledged, ranging from increased blood pressure as well as serum cholesterol increase during stress periods, to hypertension, which have far-reaching consequences such as coronary heart disease and strokes. The literature is full of firm evidence to support the link between stress and ill-health: for example, as early as 1975 health specialists warned of a relationship between illnesses such as the etiology of hypertension and stress, and more specifically we can see how 'emotional stress is generally regarded as a major factor in the etiology of hypertension' (Green et al., 1975). Similarly and very early on, in 1977 Lindemann reported an association between stress and ill-health by reporting that 33 out of 41 ulcer patients 'developed their disease in close relationship to the loss of an important person'. Others have noted a sense of utter 'helplessness' among ulcer patients and believe this feeling preceded, rather than

Table 6.1 Managers' experience of physical and psychological symptoms

Percentage who experienced	Sometimes or often 2012	Sometimes or often 2007	Change
	%	%	%
Constant tiredness	61	58	3
Insomnia/sleep loss	60	55	5
Muscular tension/ aches and pains	57	56	1
Lack of appetite or over-eating	47	48	−1
Headaches	46	45	−1
Feeling or becoming angry with others too easily	45	41	4
Having difficulty in concentrating	45	37	8
Constant irritability	37	33	4
Indigestion or heartburn	36	34	2
Loss of sense of humour	36	31	5
Avoiding contact with other people	33	25	8
Mood swings	31	27	4
Feeling unable to cope	30	25	5
Difficulty in making decisions	27	23	4
Unable to listen to other people	25	21	4
Feeling nauseous or being sick	18	15	3
Panic or anxiety attacks	15	13	2

Source: CMI Quality of Working Life (Worrall and Cooper, 2012).

resulted from, the development of ulcers. It was even stated very early on that unemployment has been shown to result in ulcers in men laid off from their jobs *and in wives* of those men (Fier, 1975, in a detailed article entitled 'Recession is causing dire illness').

Perhaps it is no coincidence therefore that global recognition by a vast array of literature since the 1970s has been associated with human health and behaviour and it is evident that when demands put upon us challenge our personal abilities to cope effectively then the consequences appear to be dire. In relation to the current world economic freeze it certainly would be interesting to monitor whether disproportionate rates of symptoms of ill-health exist in those countries that are faring worst in this economic crisis. We have already found out (Cooper et al., 2009) that there is a consistent trend in a large part of the globe for stress-related disorders to become more prevalent and severe in recent years. This is consistent with results from the Inter-Heart Study (Yusuf et al., 2004, cited in Lundberg and Cooper, 2011), a large investigation comprising 52 countries with approximately 15,000 cardiac patients and 14,000 controls in which the roles of different risk factors for chronic heart disease were evaluated. Next to cigarette smoking, psychosocial stress was found to be the most important risk factor for heart disease, increasing the risk almost three times. Stress therefore clearly exerts its effects on health in different ways and it affects bodily functions and organs, such as the cardiovascular, metabolic and immune systems. The consequence of stress, however, also influences people's life-styles, for example their dietary habits, physical activities and alcohol and tobacco consumption, and furthermore, it can increase risk-taking behaviour, causing accidents at work and in people's private lives. Stress itself is also known to have negative effects on people's compliance with treatment regimes, such as taking prescribed medication to reduce high blood pressure or following up dietary recommendations for diabetics. Another indirect consequence of occupational stress is that it can make workers less likely to use protective devices on the job, such as helmets or safety protection gear, or to follow instructions about how to use dangerous equipment in a safe way. Indeed the World Health Organization identified mental health problems and stress-related disorders as the 'the biggest overall cause of early death in Europe' (WHO, 2001, cited in Lundberg and Cooper, 2011). Given, therefore, such strong background information in relation to work, stress and health, we present below a more detailed account of the consequences of stress in relation to mental and physical wellbeing.

THE CONSEQUENCES OF STRESS: REDUCED MENTAL AND PHYSICAL WELLBEING

At the present time, we can confirm that most countries are undergoing an unprecedented economic crisis, and this has clearly taken its toll on people's health, with one in four people currently experiencing some form of psychological health problem each year (Mental Health Foundation, 2011). This worrying factor is emerging alongside given evidence that mental illness (e.g. depression, chronic fatigue syndrome, anxiety, personality disorders, drug abuse problems, schizophrenia) and pain problems are the most common reasons for individuals describing their state of health as 'poor' (Lundberg and Cooper, 2011). Although the general state of physical health has improved over an evolutionary period in most parts of the world, as reflected in longer life expectancy and more children surviving their first year of life, mental health problems as reflected in stress and lifestyle-related disorders such as anxiety, depression, burnout syndromes, Type 2 diabetes, sleep problems and diffuse muscular pains have increased dramatically at the same time. Usually physical health problems lead to mental problems, and mental problems cause deterioration in physical health. Therefore, better physical health reflected in increased life expectancy and poorer mental health seems to be a contradiction (Lundberg and Cooper, 2011). This contradiction can be explained by the fact that improved physical health, often measured in terms of infant mortality and life expectancy, during the last few decades has resulted from medical improvements, regular medical check-ups, reduced cigarette smoking in Western societies, and better health information and nutrition. Poor mental health, however, is a consequence mainly of *psychosocial* conditions – like the prevailing economic crisis – but is usually not fatal. Hence, it is possible, for example, to live a long life and suffer from a depressed mood and muscle pain, confirming that such combined effects of stressful working and social conditions will inevitably have an effect on the psychobiological functioning of the individual.

RECESSIONARY EFFECTS ON HEALTH

It has been cited that the prevalence of poor mental health in the UK is higher among the unemployed than those working full-time or part-time (OPCS, 1995), so it comes as no surprise to learn that surveys that have been conducted since the recession began are reporting higher symptoms of depression and anxiety among 48–71 per cent of those who have lost jobs, received pay cuts or had their working hours reduced, with the 18–30 age group hardest hit (cited in Weinberg and Cooper, 2012). Additionally one can note from Box 6.1 how the American Psychological Association has recently cited a corresponding increase in the number of suicides being reported in economically starved Greece and the ongoing unemployment trends, with Eurostat recently confirming (October 2013) yet another increase in unemployment trends in 16 European member states compared with a year ago in October 2012. More noticeably, the highest increases were registered in Cyprus (12.3 per cent to 16.9 per cent) and Greece

(24.6 per cent to 27.9 per cent) between June 2012 and June 2013. Not surprisingly, therefore, it has been confirmed by McManus and colleagues in 2009 that the most commonly diagnosed psychological disorders are anxiety and depression, with the most frequent of both mixed anxiety and depression being present among 9 per cent of those with a mental health problem. Psychologists are also aware that when such disorders are diagnosed, the individual is most likely to find it hard to cope with the demands of everyday life both within and outside the workplace and such problems are likely to produce even higher levels of psychological strain. Worrisome for all is the likelihood that in such situations the duration of absence from work due to poor psychological wellbeing averages a cumulative high of 26.8 working days (HSE, 2009), making the correct balance of home and work life an impossible goal to reach. Table 6.2 reports the causes of long-term absence in non-manual workers (CIPD, 2011), in which it can be seen that amongst the leading causes of absenteeism in a variety of organizations is reportedly stress and mental health problems.

However, it is important to explain here how absences in the job in addition to presenteeism and turnover are simultaneously costing industry a substantial price in these already troubled economic times. Indeed at the onset of the global recession, Sainsbury Centre for Mental Health in

Table 6.2   Causes of long-term absence: non-manual workers

Percentage of respondents citing this reason as leading cause (base 286)

	All	Manufacturing & Production	Private Services	Public Services	Non-Profit
Stress	58	38	55	70	69
Mental ill-health	46	32	50	53	43
Acute medical condition	57	61	56	59	51
Recurring medical problems	28	34	29	29	20
Back pain	50	55	41	56	57
Musculo-skeletal injury	57	61	44	73	55
Minor illness	11	4	13	14	10
Injuries/accidents not related to work	30	30	32	25	31
Home/family responsibilities	13	11	15	14	8

Source: CIPD (2011).

Table 6.3   Estimated annual costs to UK employers of mental ill-health

	Cost per average employee (£)	Total cost to UK employers (£ billion)	Per cent of total	Year
Absenteeism	335	8.4	32.4	2007
Presenteeism	605	15.1	58.4	2007
Turnover	95	2.4	9.2	2007
Total	1035	25.9	100	2007

Source: Sainsbury Centre for Mental Health (2007).

2007 reported the estimated financial costs to UK employers of mental ill-health, which can be further observed in Table 6.3.

What can certainly be concluded from the overall picture is how the consequences of occupational stress are being paid for financially, mentally and physically in a variety of ways and in a host of different countries and situations. As we have already discussed, the ongoing recession has also led to an increasing trend of 'sickness presenteeism' at work. Thus even when ill, workers will go to their job in order to show their employer that they are healthy, motivated and committed employees, who show up each day albeit sick. One must remember, however, in job-insecure times, that being 'present' is possibly perceived as a way of inoculating the individual against the next 'round' of redundancies. Furthermore, people today will go to work when feeling physically or mentally ill in order not to burden other colleagues, who are also overworked and tired, and thus may not be so willing and able to take on additional work. Indeed, Biron et al. (2006, cited in Lundberg and Cooper, 2011) investigated 9,000 employees of a Canadian governmental organization (response rate 50 per cent), and found that a high workload increased presenteeism for employees. However, what also needs to be remembered is that another important reason for sickness presenteeism, is of course, the financial loss of being absent from work. In Greece, for example, one notices that a popular 'topic of conversation' is the fear of being sick (especially amongst blue collar workers) because they may incur loss of income that is desperately relied on by the individual and family unit. In other countries, such as Sweden, for example, no economic compensation is given for the first day off work. The aim of this rule is to reduce short-term sickness absenteeism, assumed to be caused by minor health problems that are not necessarily a hindrance to work. However, as the medical profession acknowledges, being able to take a day or two off work when not feeling well may contribute to a faster recovery and reduce the risk of long-term absenteeism (Kristensen, 1991, as cited in Lundberg and Cooper, 2011).

Hansen and Andersen (2009) collected information from a random sample of 11,838 members of the Danish workforce and found that sickness presence was associated with increased long-term sickness at a later date, even after controlling for a wide range of potential confounders as well as baseline health status and previous long-term sickness absence. In addition, one must remember that going to work with a common cold or virus increases the risk that other employees will also be infected, thus causing problems for them too, and ultimately, incurring bottom-line costs for the organization.

In summary, therefore, a strong consequence of this economic crisis is that people have psychologically and physically stretched themselves to their utmost limits in order to be productive and loyal to their organization in these difficult times. Appearing at work when sick is now the norm and not the exception and will inevitably, in the long run, cause greater and more severe long-term illness.

REDUCED SOCIAL INTERACTION AND APATHY AT WORK

Given the above information it is easy to understand how people with poor mental and physical health are also likely to appear low in energy. Coupled with such symptoms is an overall lack of interest in social relationships and interactions with others. Going back to the CMI Quality of Working Life Report (Worrall and Cooper, 2012), we notice, for example, that one of the biggest symptoms reported during this recessionary period, amongst the 10,000 cohort of people, is 'avoiding contact with other people', with an 8 per cent change being reported between the years 2007 and 2012. In many incidences the exact reason for an individual experiencing such symptoms is not known, as the relationship between the causes and consequences of occupational stress can become more complex and dynamic. However, what is apparent to others is the noticeable change in a person's behaviour and attitude at work, as a general feeling of apathy and lack of motivation towards the job and people emerges. Alongside such consequences is the reduced tolerance that an individual may have of challenging situations – and it is exactly such strengths that are needed at this present time in order to effectively deal with the pressures and strains of our current turbulent world. Similar to Cannon's (1935) fight or flight syndrome, an individual who is suffering from severe strain at work often reports low energy levels and withdraws from the struggle with normal communication with others. In the long run and as extensively described by Maslach and Jackson (1986), the individual may spill over

Table 6.4   Perceived effects of organizational change on employees by level

Percentage who thought this had decreased	Director	Senior manager	Middle manager	Junior manager
	%	%	%	%
Loyalty to the organization	29	57	61	66
Morale	37	68	75	82
Motivation	32	57	65	76
Sense of job security	47	69	71	72
Wellbeing	31	54	55	63

Source: CMI Quality of Working Life (2012).

from the normal 'stress arena' to the 'strain arena' and suffer from extreme emotional strain in the form of burnout: here emotional exhaustion is evident together with a lack of personal accomplishment and depersonalization. The term 'emotional exhaustion' exemplifies exactly what this means as the individual feels 'apathetic' and 'emotionally drained'. As a consequence of such emotional strain, noticeable changes may occur in the way an individual behaves towards others; for example, a lack of consideration and respect for others are observable behaviours that may be apparent.

Coinciding with the economic recession, in 2012, again the CMI noted in their 'Quality of Working Life 2012: Managers' Wellbeing, Motivation and Productivity report' (Worrall and Cooper, 2012), how organizations which have recently undergone a change show a noticeable difference in managers' perceptions of the job. Table 6.4 reports the perceived effects of organizational change on employees by level.

In summary, and as has been shown in our Dynamics of work stress model (Figure 5.1, Chapter 5), additional and serious consequences can emerge in the form of altered behaviour – and this may range from reduced social interaction and apathy at work, to low morale and loyalty to the organization. Perhaps it could be suggested that in these difficult times individuals have become confused in terms of who they can turn to, and who they can possibly trust, and therefore communication is kept to a bare minimum. All in all, it can be agreed, that at the individual level the consequences of occupational stress are severe and far from being eliminated in this changing world.

THE COSTS OF STRAIN AT THE ORGANIZATIONAL LEVEL

In simple terms it must be remembered that all organizations, in all countries, are nothing more than 'an entity of human beings' and therefore at any given time an organization will act as a mirror and reflect how employees feel. Having identified at the beginning of this chapter how an *individual* may display symptoms of strain, it is now important to recognize how strain may also become apparent at the *organizational* level. For example, in terms of the workplace, The European Agency for Safety and Health at Work (cited Cooper, 2012), recently published their second European-wide opinion poll on Occupational Safety and Health (www.osha.europa. eu), which surveyed over 35,000 workers in 36 European countries. As a consequence of the continuing recession and downturn 77 per cent of respondents said they thought job-related stress would increase over the next five years, with only 7 per cent saying they thought it was likely to decrease. Indeed, one could say that this is not really surprising, given the tough conditions currently being experienced in Europe and beyond. As already discussed in chapters 4 and 5, most people are being challenged with having 'to do more with less', in times of insecurity, greater demands, and abrasive and conflicting managerial styles. Furthermore, and in alignment with the Dynamics of work stress model (Figure 5.1, Chapter 5), a host of issues may prevail and these issues may refer to things that are not 'tangible' and cannot be 'seen', such as absenteeism and turnover as well as presenteeism. These are symptoms that are more subtle but nonetheless they have a strong and negative impact on the functioning and economic strength of a company. For example, in the United Kingdom, 40 per cent of all absenteeism is attributed to psychological health problems, and this is currently costing the nation £8.4 billion (Sainsbury Centre for Mental Health, 2007).

As mentioned in the beginning of this chapter, economic problems in one country will certainly have ripple effects in other countries, and indeed in both Germany and the Netherlands the cost of sickness absence due to poor psychological health has been estimated to be in the region of approximately 3 billion euros (Houtman, 2005). In an earlier study, Elkin and Rosch (1990) provided statistics for the United States, revealing that psychological strain related to work has been estimated to coincide with 54 per cent of absenteeism and is currently costing American organizations billions of dollars (CCH, Unscheduled Absence Survey, 2007). Moreover, and according to the UK National Institute for Clinical Excellence (NICE, 2009), 13 in every 1000 employees resign from their jobs each year due to psychological ill-health and this has an accompanying replacement cost

Table 6.5   The costs of workplace stress and mental health problems

1. Total cost to employers of mental ill-health at work is estimated at £29.5 billion per annum[1]
2. Stress from work per annum costs employers an estimated £3.7 billion[2]
3. 13m working days are lost[3]
4. Total cost of incapacity benefit per annum is £12 billion[4]
5. Nearly 40% of people drawing incapacity benefit (IB) have a mental health condition = £5 billion

Cost of stress in the workplace results from a wide range of sources such as:

● sickness absence;
● labour turnover;
● premature retirement;
● health insurance;
● treatment of consequences of stress.

Notes:
1. Sainsbury Centre for Mental Health (2008).
2. Confederation of British Industry (CBI) (2005).
3. Health and Safety Committee (HSC) (2004).
4. Department for Work and Pensions (DWP) (2006).

Source: Lundberg and Cooper (2011). *Government Office for Science*, Department for Innovation, Universities and Skills (DIUS).

which ranges from £3,150 to £9,000, depending on the type of employment and job function of the individual. Similarly, recent evidence tells us that the total cost of replacing employees who are under such strain at work is estimated to be at a huge £2.4 billion each year (Sainsbury Centre for Mental Health, 2007) and in light of such evidence it is certain to say that the impact of forced cutbacks and economic poverty due to the recession is forecast to compound this problem severely. Table 6.5 reports the true costs of workplace stress and mental health problems in the UK, as cited by Lundberg and Cooper (2011).

In the previous chapter, and above, we discussed the increasingly rec-ognized problem of presenteeism at work, which clearly has accelerated in tandem with the worldwide crisis. As mentioned, it appears that employees are turning up to work even if they are not well, and in an explanation of this it has been claimed (Cooper, 2013) that the individual continues to work out of fear of losing their job in times of high job insecurity. Here it needs to be said that whilst the individual is certainly suffering by working when under par, the organization is also paying dearly for reduced productivity. As previously mentioned, and as a reminder to readers, in

2004 Goetzel and colleagues estimated that presenteeism costs four or five times more than absenteeism, and, more specifically, Sainsbury Mental Health report in 2007 estimated the annual cost to be as high as £15.1 billion. Table 6.3 highlights these costs and acts as a reminder to readers of the continued organizational costs of strain which appear to have increased in recent years. As analytically stated by The Sainsbury Centre for Mental Health (2007):

> The measurement for presenteeism is difficult, but accumulating international evidence suggests that such losses in on-the-job productivity may be several times larger than the losses caused by sickness absence. . . The average cost of presenteeism is put at around £145 per working day lost, corresponding to the average gross daily compensation of employees in the UK economy.

In addition to the abovementioned problems embedded at the organizational level, one must also note how the frequency of work stoppages appears to have increased with the economic downturn. In most European countries and at any particular point in time we hear in the news how employees are either striking, or working with stoppages, to demonstrate a displeasing aspect or outcome of their employment contract. Simply, all strikes and work stoppages are initiated by people who are desperately unhappy at work and therefore display their 'dissatisfaction' outwardly and collectively. However, such collective action is simultaneously being paid for by industries in the form of production loss, inefficiency and loss of income. Noteworthy is the fact that strikes and work stoppages are frequently visible in many countries both within and outside Europe. For example, and as stated in Box 6.1, it is interesting to see that the International Labour Organization states: 'From Tahrir Square to Wall Street, growing economic inequalities and a persistent lack of jobs have caused demonstrators in many countries to demand real change from their governments. But as the global economic recovery stalls and high unemployment rates persist, the root causes of social unrest shows no signs of abating' (ILO, July 2013). Furthermore in more distant cultures like China a similar picture is emerging, where in July 2013 it was claimed that: 'For China, the next three months will bring more layoffs, bankruptcies, protests and trade frictions' (STRATFOR, Third Quarter Forecast, July 2013). More specifically and as will be discussed further on, such strikes are highly likely to lead to general social unrest.

Logic dictates that with such accumulating stressors occurring and in these times of economic difficulty the likelihood of company failure becomes greater. Similar to being caught up in a whirlwind, a company becomes locked in a scenario with unsolvable problems. For example, as documented by STRATFOR Global Intelligence (August 2013), the European economic crisis continues to hurt Spanish companies, and during the first half of 2013 there was a record number of bankruptcies, especially by small and medium-sized enterprises in the construction and industry sectors. The Spanish National Statistics Institute issued a warning on the position of the Spanish economy on 7 August 2013, when it revealed that 5,069 companies had filed for bankruptcy during the first half of 2013, a 22.5 per cent increase from the first half of 2012 and the highest number since the statistical series began in 2004. Clearly the construction sector, with predominately blue collar workers, has been hardest hit by the crisis; roughly 27 per cent of all the bankruptcies filed between January and June 2013 involved construction companies. However, other sectors such as retail (which accounted for 17.7 per cent of the bankruptcies) and industry and energy (17.3 per cent), are also particularly affected by the economic crisis in the eurozone's fourth largest economy (STRATFOR, 8 August 2013). Admittedly Spain is just one example of many countries that can be cited: however, what can be concluded is that as the crisis continues, the consequences are immense and are simultaneously being paid for by individuals, organizations and most societies. Coupled with continued stagnation and high unemployment, the fundamental belief in prosperity can be questioned, and hence, with the current situations as stated above, it seems highly likely that social unrest will soar and that repairing the economic and social fabric will become a very long-term goal indeed.

THE COSTS OF STRAIN AT THE SOCIETAL LEVEL

The costs of strain at the societal level can be expressed in many ways and are primarily studied by sociologists and/or social anthropologists. However, in alignment with our model (Figure 5.1), emphasis is given to two social issues that we believe play a fundamental role in the relationship between the individual and industry: unemployment issues and corresponding social unrest.

It comes as no surprise to document that these two social issues have increased in severity in recent years and the general outcome regarding improvements in most societies is still doubtful. In November 2013, the comments emerging from STRATFOR Global Intelligence are 'Unemployment will remain at critically high levels' (6 November, 2013), whilst it is forecast that 'The European crisis is far from over. . .Even if some economies grow next year, the political consequences of high unemployment would still be felt for years to come' (STRATFOR, 6 November, 2013). Captured in this ongoing economic crisis, which began

Table 6.6   Composition of the Social Unrest Index

Confidence in government	35%
Living standard	20%
Freedom in your life	20%
Local job market	20%
Internet access	5%

Source: ILO (2013).

almost six years ago, the forecast for job opportunities and social stability is still somewhat bleak. The authors therefore predict that given the above specified problems, and as discussed throughout this chapter, an ongoing pattern of unemployment and turbulence at work will continue in the near future and may give rise to the sensitivies of social unrest. More specifically and recently analysed by The International Labour Organization (ILO, 2013), a similar voice is heard from their recent report:

> This latest report found that, since the global crisis, social unrest had increased in a majority of economies. Insufficient economic growth and high unemployment rates are the two most important determinants. Youth unemployment, like all unemployment, increases social unrest, but the impact of total unemployment on social unrest was actually larger than the effect of youth unemployment, specifically.

Table 6.6 shows the composition of the Social Unrest Index, taken from the World of Work Report (ILO, 2013). More specifically the index is constructed using variables drawn from the Gallup World Poll Survey and relates to respondents' confidence in government, standard of living, personal freedoms, job opportunities and access to the Internet. According to the ILO 2013 World of Work Report, it is claimed that: 'The ILO has reported increase in social unrest using its social unrest index, a composite indicator which provides a reflection of national social health'.

Furthermore and in this latest report, the majority of advanced, developing and emerging economies have all 'witnessed increases in social unrest as a result of the crisis'. But more specifically, 'advanced countries have, on average, had the highest social unrest index score'. The conclusion of this report is also interesting and confirms that: 'Among the advanced economies, Europe is more likely to face social unrest than is North America or other non-EU advanced economies, which is likely a result of policy responses to the ongoing sovereign debt crisis and impacts on people's lives and perceptions of well-being'.

With unemployment at a European and member state level still increasing, the consequences in terms of overall strain and wellbeing for employees and most citizens in Europe remain worrisome. Given the concrete statistical evidence that is provided by Eurostat (October, 2013), it is currently estimated that 26.595 million men and women in the EU-28, of whom 19.178 million were in the euro area (EA-17), were unemployed in August 2013. These results are severe, extremely high and not optimistic in the short-term range. According to Eurostat (October, 2013), compared with August 2012, unemployment rose by 882,000 in the EU-28 and by 895,000 in the euro area.

Given that statistics 'tell us and sell us facts', the realities show us that unemployment trends and the economic crisis remains well embedded in most societies in Europe. Similarly in the United States, economists are reporting a correspondingly bleak picture: for example the Economic Research and Investment Strategy (INSIGHT, October 2013) reports that 'the labor market suffers from the persistent high levels of long term unemployed'.

An additional sign of job weakness and the erosion effects it has on society is shown by the large number of people who want to work full-time but are only offered part-time positions – 'working part-time for economic reasons' is the Bureau of Labor Statistics' term in the United States (as cited in Economic Research and Investment Strategy, October 2013). However, for economists and organizational psychologists, this obviously reflects a hidden caution by employers to contain costs, as part-time workers do not have the legal rights or pension benefits enjoyed by full-time workers. Moreover, recovery in terms of re-employment opportunities is not equal across all occupation types, and as noticed in America, for example, new jobs tend to be in the sectors of leisure, hospitality, retailing, fast-food, and other low-paying industries. Finally, and of extreme concern, is the fact that economists have noticed that this particular world recession is taking much longer to recover than other global recessions in the past and as boldly stated by the Economic Research and Investment Strategy (October 2013): 'As of August 2013, 67 months after the payroll peak in January 2008, jobs are still 1.9 million below the top while in earlier recoveries, the earlier peak was bested much earlier'.

Hence, the idea that the general public have that 'recovery is taking place', may in fact be a myth told to people in order to sustain social stability and calmness overall. For economists, however, who are keeping track of all trends and statistics, this may not be the true case and a worrisome picture has emerged. Taken together, one can now see how the consequences of the changing economic landscape are giving rise to problems in society and overall social stability. For example, in a recent national survey of UK families, the Centre for the Modern Family (2012) (cited in Cooper, 2012), it was found that as a consequence of the recession, 78 per cent of the sample population felt that family life is tougher now than it was before the recession, with 20 per cent reporting that they were struggling to cope financially, and another 39 per cent 'just getting by'. Indeed, only 7 per cent of the UK sample population was finding family life comfortable at present. In addition, three times as many families are saying that their financial problems are a more significant cause of stress than the pressures of bringing up children. What can be concluded is that by going through such extremely turbulent economic times, and for such a long period – currently spanning over six years of turbulence, the fabric of most nation states has been adversely affected and their ability to survive and grow in the near future is questionable.

SUMMARY

Given the fact that high unemployment continues around the globe, this issue should be a top concern for economists, organizational and social psychologists as well as governments as a whole. Apart from its financial and social effects on personal life, unemployment and continued disruption in the job market negatively affects social cohesion, and ultimately will continue to hinder economic growth and the wellbeing of its citizens. Unemployment, social unrest and company failures are clearly important indicators of the overall wellbeing of people. Time and time again, the effects of unemployment with its corrosive impact on families and communities has been well documented (Black, 2008). The psychological challenges experienced by the individual facing the reality of a job loss, as well as the difficulties endured by others – families and friends and households in general – are immense. The authors claim that the psychological difficulties are not only financial, but the support and resources available to the individual who is without employment are limited, making overall strain immense. In summary, the effects of not working are directly related to health and wellbeing, and furthermore, damaging working environments have impacts which are far-reaching, both emotionally, and with regard to practical considerations. In conclusion, therefore, we again emphasize to the reader that 'the economic crisis and occupational stress' are strongly bonded and fused. The realities of closures and organizational cutbacks diminish the chances of gaining new employment. It is these realities that play a major part in the psyche of each individual, which is further affected by this ongoing economic crisis and stress in times of a changing world.

CONCLUSION

Throughout this book the authors have discussed several fundamental issues. On the one hand, and despite the fact that we are not economists, we have devoted a component of this book (Part I) to economic affairs. We did so as the authors believe that any major changes in economic activities are highly likely to cause disruption in the working environment and thus create undue stress amongst all employees and most likely amongst all sectors of the working population – both white-collar workers, blue-collar workers and in the public and private sector. We have also highlighted to the reader how until very recently, few researchers and scientists have attempted to look at both economic affairs and psychological consequences through one prism: rather, both domains have been studied in isolation. We believe that the time has now come for both economic factors and psychological factors to be combined, and as we have shown in Part II of this book, they are clearly interdependent. Furthermore, we would like to suggest that for efficient work and economic solutions to be found, there is a vital need for both economic activities and psychological work-related issues to be assessed in combination.

Secondly, we have shown, using accurate historical traces and statistical evidence, that global recessions are not unheard-of phenomena; on the contrary, they appear to have cyclical patterns. However, as we have discussed throughout this book, there are indeed elements of this current world economic crisis that are simply unique, and thus have created great turbulence in the world of work and for those in it. For example, world economists have been faced with the invention of the euro, which has proven to have great imbalances due to the competitive powers and varying economic positions of different nations. At the same time, these unique economic problems are also creating unusual stressors in the working environment and societies at large: such is the case that organizational psychologists are now confronted with a host of problems that were not evident in the past and now need to be addressed. Needless to say, and as shown in this chapter, the overall psychological and physical wellbeing of the employee is currently at high risk.

Finally and as shown in Part I of this book, it is truly incorrect to suggest that world economies were unprepared for such a crisis and/or that governments were unaware that such negative factors were present. However, we acknowledge that given the unique factors present in this economic crisis, it is making the turnaround point extremely difficult to attain and the recovery phase much longer than anticipated. Thus, in conclusion, we agree that given the economic problems that are firmly embedded in most societies, full recovery is still a long way off and yet at the same time we strongly believe that there is a need to address the psychological functioning of the individual and, where possible, offer suitable solutions to the prevailing and ongoing stressors of our current times.

REFERENCES

Black, C. (2008). Working for a healthier tomorrow: Review of the health of Britain's working age population. Presented to the Secretary of State for Health and the Secretary of State for Works and Pensions. London: The Stationery Office. As cited in P. Dewe, M. O'Driscoll and C. Cooper eds, *Coping with Work Stress: A Review and Critique*, Chichester: Wiley-Blackwell.

Bloomberg (2013). EU: Car sales drop to lowest recorded level, 17 September, Bloomberg.com.

Cannon, W.B. (1935). Stresses and strains of homeostasis. *American Journal of Medical Science*, 189 (1), 1–14.

CCH (2007). Unscheduled Absence Survey. Available at http://hr.cch.com.press/releases.

Chartered Institute of Personnel Development (CIPD) (2011). Absence Management Annual Survey, produced in partnership with simplyhealth, available at: www.cipd.co.uk/research/_absence-managment.

Cooper, C.L. (2012). Stress in turbulent economic times. *Stress & Health*. Wiley Online Library. Available at: onlinelibrary.wiley.comcom.

Cooper, C.L. (2013). 'UK has a cultural problem of "overworking"', says HR thinker Cary Cooper, *HR Magazine*, 16 May, available at: http://www.hrmagazine.co.uk/hro/news/1077237/uk-cultural-overworking-hr-thinker-cary.

Cooper, C.L., Field, J., Goswami, U., Jenkins, R. and Sahakian, B. (eds) (2009). *Mental Capital and Wellbeing*. Oxford: Wiley-Blackwell.

Elkin, A.J. and Rosch, P.J. (1990). Promoting mental health at the workplace: The prevention side of stress management. *Occupational Medicine: State of the Art Review*, 5 (4), 739–54.

Eurostat (10 July 2013). Unemployment statistics. Available at: http://epp.eurostat.ee.europa.eu/statistics _explained/index.php.

Fier, B. (1975). Recession is causing dire illness. *Moneysworth*, 23 June.

Goetzel, R., Long, S., Oziminkowski, R., Hawkins, K., Wang, S. and Lynch, W. (2004). Health, absence, disability and presenteeism cost estimates of certain physical and mental health conditions affecting US employers. *Journal of Occupational and Environmental Medicine*, 46, 398–412.

Green, L.W., Levine, D.M. and Deeds, S. (1975). Clinical trials of health education for hypertensive outpatients: Design and baseline data. *Preventive Medicine* 4, 417–25.

The Guardian (2013). Bank of America intern's death put banks' working culture in spotlight, 21 August, *The Guardian*.

Hansen, C.D. and Andersen, J.H. (2009). Sick at work: a risk factor for long-term sickness absence at a later date? *Journal of Epidemiology and Community Health*, 63 (5), 397–402.

Health and Safety Executive (HSE) (2009). Stress-related and psychological disorders: Summary, available at: www.hse.gov.uk/statistics.causedis/stress/index.htm.

Houtman, I. (2005). Work-related stress. European Foundation for the Improvement of Living and Working Conditions. Available at: http://www/eurofound.europa.eu/ewco/reports.

INSIGHT (October, 2013). Economic Research and Investment Strategy: Gary Shilling's INSIGHT, XXIX (10), available at: www.agaryshilling.com.

International Labour Organization (ILO) (8 July 2013). Are economic stagnation and unemployment fueling social unrest? http://www.ilo.org/newyork/voices -at work/WCMS_217280/lang--en/index.htm.

International Labour Organization (ILO) (2013). World of Work Report 2013, ILO.

Kathimerini (2013). Care homes see mass exodus: thousands of Greek families opting to take family members out of nursing facilities, *International Herald Tribune*, English edn, 18 September, available at: www.ekathimerini.com.

Lindemann, E. (1977). Symptomatology and management of acute grief, in Alan Monat and Richard S. Lazarus (eds), *Stress and Coping: An Anthology*, New York: Columbia University Press.

Lundberg, U. and Cooper, C.L. (2011). *The Science of Occupational Health: Stress, Psychobiology and the New World of Work*. Chichester: Wiley-Blackwell.

Maslach, C. and Jackson, S. (1986). *The Maslach Burnout Inventory Manual*. Palo Alto: Consulting Psychologists Press.

McManus, S., Meltzer, H., Brugha, T., Bebbington, P. and Jenkins, R. (2009). *Adult Psychiatric Morbidity in England, 2007: Results of a Household Survey*. Leeds: NHS Information Centre.

Mental Health Foundation (2011). Mental health statistics: The most common mental health problems. Available at: http://www.mental-health.org.uk/help-information/mental-health-statistics/common-mental-health problems/.

National Institute for Health and Clinical Excellence (NICE) (November, 2009). Available at: http://www.nice.org.uk/nicemedia/pdf/PH22Guidance.pdf.

OPCS (1995). *Office of Population Census and Surveys British Household Psychiatric Survey*. London: HMSO.

Sainsbury Centre for Mental Health (2007). Mental health at work: Developing the business case. Policy Paper No. 8. London: Sainsbury Centre for Mental Health.

STRATFOR (May 2013). Youth unemployment in the European Union. *STRATFOR Global Intelligence*, 29 May, available at: www.stratfor.com.

STRATFOR (July 2013). Third Quarter Forecast 2013. *STRATFOR Global Intelligence*, 9 July, available at: www.stratfor.com.

STRATFOR (8 August 2013). In Spain, bankruptcies undermine economic growth. *STRATFOR Global Intelligence*, available at: www.stratfor.com.

STRATFOR (14 August 2013). The Eurozone: Out of recession but not out of trouble: *STRATFOR Global Intelligence*, available at: www.stratfor.com.

STRATFOR (18 September 2013). The end of the welfare state in Europe? STRATFOR Global Intelligence, available at: www.stratfor.com.

STRATFOR (23 September 2013). In Germany, Merkel will seek a new coalition, STRATFOR Global Intelligence, available at: www.stratfor.com.

STRATFOR (6 November 2013). Manifestations of the European crisis, STRATFOR Global Intelligence, available at: www.stratfor.com.

Theorell, T. (2011). Unhealthy Work, 1 April, available at: Unhealthyworkblog. blogspot.com.

Weinberg, A. and Cooper, C.L. (2012). *Stress in Turbulent Times*. Basingstoke: Palgrave Macmillan.

Worrall, L. and Cooper, C.L. (2012). *The Quality of Working Life 2012*: *Managers' Wellbeing, Motivation and Productivity*. London: Chartered Management Institute (CMI).

PART III

Post economic crisis – from sustainability to wellbeing

7.   Organizational effectiveness and wellbeing at work: post economic crisis

INTRODUCTION

Throughout this book, the authors have shown how each and every one of us has been affected by this ongoing economic crisis, which unfortunately has just entered its sixth year of immense turmoil with few signs of abating. As we have discussed, with high levels of job insecurity evident, coupled with increasing demands on people to work harder and for longer hours, and given a more robust and abrasive managerial style, the overall changing landscape of the working environment is far from satisfactory. During the last six years, and around the globe, we have witnessed huge economic and financial upheavals, making it now certain that this ongoing recession has had a negative impact on most citizens in terms of their psychological and physical wellbeing. Starting with the banking crash in America in 2008 (and as discussed in Part I of this book), which led to the domino effects of low growth and high unemployment in most countries (as discussed in Part II of this book), we can now confirm that as a result the whole working sector has now been severely affected. Professors Les Worrall and Cary Cooper surveyed a cohort of 10,000 UK managers, from shop floor to top floor, in their Quality of Working Life report (2012) and found that the current negative economic and financial position of most organizations is immense, causing a deterioration in wellbeing measures and low productivity. Furthermore, and as stated from their research findings: 'The effect of five years of recession, low growth and austerity on managers' wellbeing in UK business has been profound across all types of business...Our findings raise significant questions about how well UK business organisations are being managed in these difficult times'.

Given these crystal clear answers, the profound effects of these difficult times are now being felt in most countries and organizations on an escalating scale. With acute and chronic stressors firmly in place, we believe that it is vitally important – and probably more so than ever before – to fully utilize our coping strategies in an attempt to reinstate wellness and happiness at work. However, before we begin to review the various coping strategies at work and suggest their current applicability in today's turbulent workforce, we emphasize and recognize that in these difficult economic times companies are bound to make structural reforms and cutbacks in order to survive. Nonetheless, it is the *way* that management deals with such difficulties that concerns us, and when improved productivity is achieved in a harsh and unsympathetic way, or when employees are 'bypassed' in important decisions concerning their physical and psychological welfare, then this is of immediate concern, and as such, it should not be allowed to be pursued at any cost.

REVIEW OF COPING STRATEGIES AT WORK: ASSESSING METHODOLOGICAL ISSUES

Simultaneously, we acknowledge that, given the changing work context that has resulted from this economic crisis, the coping strategies that were once utilized and relied upon may not be so applicable today. Furthermore, it is important to draw attention to the fact that while instruments for measuring work stressors are available, and have been available for a long period of time, their applicability in today's turbulent world is also questionable. In addition, and as stated by Dewe et al. (2012), the considerable economic and social change that has occurred since many stressor measures were first developed has meant that these measures may now be prone to an 'inherent bias', where we overemphasize the importance of some stressor events, ignore others and fail to consider the significance of such stressors to the individual. Such serious omissions therefore need to be addressed. Thus, when it comes to measuring stressors today, one must be careful that the issue is relevant, and furthermore, the measures being used must accurately capture those stressors and those events that correctly and currently reflect the economic and organizational position on an international scale. Indeed earlier on in the literature, Dewe and Kompier (2008) suggest that there has been a profound change across all aspects of society, and that the landscape of work and society has been influenced by three prevailing forces: internationalization and global competition; technological advances; and demographic shifts in the workforce, which have influenced work patterns and work stressors of our times. Therefore, and as suggested by Dewe et al. in later work (2010), understanding the coping literature is not just about stressors; it is also about how we define stress, how we capture that experience in research, what measures we use, whose reality those measures express, how researchers interpret their results and how this knowledge contributes to theory, practice and those whose working lives we study (Dewe et al., 2010, p. 23).

In the assessment of the coping materials and issues raised below, we encourage the reader to be fully aware of the position of the current coping research, and to understand the complex and changing nature of our working environments. Indeed, some solutions and recommendations shown below may only be partially of use to some organizations and employees, and how effective their coping is really depends on the inter-action between the person and the environment, or the well-established interactionist perspective to the stress–strain phenomenon under study. Nonetheless, and in summary, we also suggest that it is indeed this complexity and these changes that will also influence in which direction the individual, organization and researchers will go in the future, in an attempt to improve wellbeing, effectiveness and efficiency in all employ-ment sectors.

PROMOTING WELLBEING AND HEALTH AT WORK

Starting with the organizational level, there is an abundance of literature, spanning approximately 30 years of research (Dewe et al., 2010), which has compiled evidence about the conditions of work and management that help to promote health and wellbeing. Whilst such accumulating evidence has been of great importance in the past, it must be remembered that the current ongoing work stressors are indeed unique, thereby making the 'usual' coping strategies and remedies not so relevant and applicable during recessionary periods. What we do know, however, is that in order to maintain a healthy workforce, an organization, with its management, has a great ethical, moral and legal responsibility to look after its staff, and at all economic times – both good and bad. Thus, given today's economic problems, all companies should take on the additional responsibility for the working lives of its employees so that each individual can be better equipped to counter the increased and acute stressors that are prevailing during these difficult economic and social times. According to a recent report published in *The Sunday Times* (March 2013), the message is clear: 'Support your staff and they will support you'. In the thirteenth annual survey conducted by *The Sunday Times* on the '100 Best Companies to Work For in 2013', extensive results regarding employee engagement were revealed. More specifically: 'The levels of workplace engagement required to make the grade as a "best company to work for" are high, but bring significant business benefits'.

In other words, in order to maximize organizational effectiveness and efficiency, an organization needs to put in place coping strategies to assist both the company *and* its workforce. To set the benchmark, and as stated in the survey:

> Enlightened and forward-looking business leaders, such as the ones revealed in the list, are investing in the wellbeing and motivation of their most valuable assets: their employees. And in a tough economic climate this makes sense. The inspiring quality of their workplace culture is not just an add-on benefit: it's a crucial ingredient for competitiveness and sustainable growth.

Table 7.1 lists the various categories that this survey taps into regarding the key issues of importance, as rated by employees.

From the recent report, and in summary, it is noted that having a supportive manager, understanding colleagues, and job security are vitally important predictors of good mental health in the job and this cannot be underestimated. However, we acknowledge that no amount of positive practice appears to be able to hold back the devastation and disruption that this economic crisis has brought us, yet at the same time organizations must begin to get to grips with the new challenges of our eras. By facing the challenges in these difficult times it may be possible to bring about change

Table 7.1   The Sunday Times 100 Best Companies to Work For

Categories and criteria:	
LEADERSHIP	How employees feel about the head of a company and its senior management
WELLBEING	How staff feel about the stress, pressure and balance between work and home duties
GIVING SOMETHING BACK	How much companies are thought by their staff to put back into society generally and the local community
PERSONAL GROWTH	To what extent staff feel they are stretched and challenged by their job
MY MANAGER	How staff feel towards their immediate boss and day-to-day managers
MY COMPANY	Feelings about the company people work for as opposed to the people they work with
MY TEAM	How staff feel about their immediate colleagues
FAIR DEAL	How happy the workforce is with their pay and benefits

Source: The Sunday Times (2014).

which will then incorporate flexibility to improve the organization, engage the workers and empower staff. The outcomes of such changes will most likely include greater levels of trust, security and productive behaviour in the company, and therefore it is vital that we do not leave organizations to their 'fate' or expect a miracle to occur. As such, we have outlined below various approaches and strategies that we believe organizations can utilize in order to further maximize effectiveness and wellbeing in the job during these extremely difficult, *although not impossible*, economic times.

According to Weinberg and Cooper (2012), organizational approaches to wellbeing at work involve a combination of organizational interventions which should provide a portfolio of employee-friendly options that simultaneously benefit the organization. More specifically, they claim that a 'three-pronged approach' to organizational health is warranted, which combines prevention, management and treatment options to tackle the immediate concerns of the day as well as to lay the foundations for a longer-term strategy for employee wellbeing. Shown below is this triangular approach (as cited in Weinberg and Cooper, 2012; Robertson and Cooper, 2011; Cartwright and Cooper, 2011).

- *Primary interventions* which focus on the *prevention of problems arising in the first place*: for example, considerate and compassionate management, with clear communication strategies, which are essential during organizational change, participative job redesign, promoting organizational citizenship and management coaching.
- *Secondary interventions* aim to manage the *symptoms of strain* and associated problems by targeting the *individual* in the workplace: for example, stress management programmes, such as relaxation techniques, stress management techniques, assertiveness training, interview skills and job-seeking workshops and coaching initiatives.
- *Tertiary interventions* are designed to *help the individual* who may need more specialized input to deal with the strain: for example, employee assistance programmes offering counselling.

According to the World Health Organization 'a healthy working environment is one in which there is not only an absence of harmful conditions, but an abundance of health promoting ones' (Leka et al., 2007). More recently (2012), and noted by 'Simplyhealth – we can be bothered' (Simplyhealth, 2012): 'There is also a moral aspect to improving employees wellbeing. If organisations expect high levels of commitment and motivation, they have a duty to develop a culture and environment that fosters wellbeing'.

This above statement clearly places the responsibility on the employer to be proactive in creating a healthy and fit environment with suitable conditions for all employees to work in. With the average employee spending approximately one third of the life in their occupation, a healthy environment is a vital component for overall wellbeing. Amongst the top 100 companies to work for, as reviewed by *The Sunday Times* Survey (January 2014), employees picked their top companies for 'leadership, job security and future prospects', as well as 'enlightened employers are motivating staff by keeping them up-to-date about plans for the future'.

Given today's recessionary period, a correct and adequate management style that is open and honest with its workforce is likely to succeed. As Bradon (2009) states: 'Good leadership has the largest influence on employee engagement' and, therefore, it is apparent that during these difficult and turbulent periods it is vital that organizations support their staff if they are to succeed.

IMPORTANT CRITERIA FOR SUSTAINABILITY AND WELLBEING

It was approximately ten years ago that the Health and Safety Executive Board (HSE) in the United Kingdom introduced a set of standards for managing stress in the organization. For readers who are unfamiliar with the HSE, it is a government appointed body in the United Kingdom (HSE, 2009); more specifically, it offers guidance and support from upper level management for related initiatives. It should be remembered and noted from our previous chapter that indeed 40 per cent of sickness absence according to Sainsbury Centre for Mental Health (2007) is attributed to sickness absence due to psychological health issues. Similarly in a study conducted by Professors Les Worrall and Cary Cooper (2006), in partnership with the Chartered Management Institute and funded by Simplyhealth, an insight was given into what was happening to UK managers and organizational wellbeing just before the 2007/8 crash as the biggest boom we have ever had turned into the biggest collapse in recent history. The same survey five years on (2012) reported some dismal findings such as:

- There was a marked increase in managers reporting that they were suffering from stress or depression with a deterioration being recorded on 12 of their 13 health and wellbeing measures.
- The deterioration in wellbeing measures was particularly marked on measures that affected managers' ability to do their jobs effectively (e.g. feeling unable to cope and feeling anxious).

- There had been an organizational hardening in attitudes to ill-health, with fewer managers feeling that they were treated sympathetically by their organizations if they had time off ill; the percentage feeling that organizations were not doing enough to support employee well-being also showed an increase. (Worrall and Cooper, 2012)

Similarly, in the United States the National Institute for Occupational Health and Safety has run its own research programme since 1996 to support the dissemination of advice and research findings for organizations and employees. Below, we outline the six psychosocial aspects of work highlighted by the UK's HSE as directly impacting on our wellbeing:

1. DEMANDS: this is tapping into employees' workloads, specific patterns of work and the physical nature of the working environment in relation to whether employees feel able to cope with the demands placed upon them. More specifically, in England and the UK generally, the HSE-stipulated standards require that a system exist in the organization to address concerns and possible problems revolving around workload, and it is stipulated that all employees be provided with 'adequate and achievable demands in relation to the agreed hours of work', and furthermore that their skills and abilities be closely matched to their job demands and function.
2. CONTROL: employees should 'have a say about the way they do their work', and 'where possible have control over their pace of work'. Indeed as early as 1998, a key finding in relation to occupational stress and job satisfaction, in a community-wide survey conducted in the United Kingdom amongst approximately 2500 workers representing all socio-economic groups, a key predictor of job satisfaction was found to be autonomy and control in the job (Fotinatos-Ventouratos and Cooper, 1998).
3. SUPPORT: sponsoring and encouragement should be provided by the organization to its workers, and information should be given by staff. Indeed as we have suggested throughout our book, it is vitally important that employees are 'not left in the dark', with a lack of consultation and information. Furthermore, the HSE directly recommends that working patterns be matched and monitored, with adequate rest periods and breaks being given, in addition to opportunities to develop new skills being encouraged and supported. When employee development and success is ensured, constructive feedback should also be given.
4. RELATIONSHIPS: positive behaviour should be complemented by policies and procedures for reporting and dealing with unacceptable behaviour in the workplace such as bullying and harassment at work.

5. ROLE: staff need to be directly and clearly informed about their job function and they should not be placed in a role in which performing a task causes conflict for those individuals. However, and admittedly while this may be unavoidable at times and in various situations, correct systems and policies should be in place to address 'role conflict'.

6. CHANGE: this involves informing and engaging employees by providing opportunities for them to influence proposals for change. Employees should be made aware of the potential outcomes of the change process, and there is a responsibility for employers to provide suitable training and support to help staff adjust. This may be particularly relevant during downsizing or restructuring prompted by the economic recession (HSE, 2009, cited in Weinberg and Cooper, 2012).

Similarly and as stated in 'Simplyhealth' (Cooper, 2012), it has been suggested that 'when creating wellbeing strategies in the workplace, buy in from the top to start with is vital'. It is suggested that the board and senior management teams need to be won over to the cause. The best approach, it is believed, is a 'blend of a strong business case, populated by information and data from your organisation, and an appeal to more emotional reasoning in senior people'. This quote, provided by Cooper (2012), clearly encompasses the majority of the six strategies above as stated and outlined in work by the HSE, thus creating a picture and coherent whole of what prosperity will look like, and how success may unfold.

In the not so distant past, the UK's Foresight project on mental capital and wellbeing (2008) carried out an analysis identifying economic gains which could be made by taking an organizational approach to stress and wellbeing (as cited in Weinberg and Cooper, 2012). Their initial projections highlighted great benefits from auditing the psychological health of employees, which they estimated to be around £100 million per annum (National Institute for Clinical Excellence (NICE), 2009). Furthermore, and beyond this, the Foresight commission predicts that the implementation of strategies to prevent mental ill-health at work would save £275 million. More recently, Robertson and Flint-Taylor (as cited in Cartwright and Cooper, 2011) adopted a framework around which to build organizational outcomes, utilizing a '6 essentials' of workplace wellbeing, which are: resources and communication; control; balanced workload; job security and change; work relationships; and job conditions. These factors drive psychological wellbeing, which in turn feeds through to individual and organizational outcomes. Table 7.2 shows this framework.

It is acknowledged that developing a culture that fosters employee wellbeing is important; however, as Cooper (2012) states:

Table 7.2   A '6 essentials' approach to workplace wellbeing

6 Essentials	Psychological wellbeing	Individual outcomes	Organizational outcomes
Resource & Communication	Sense of purpose	Productivity & satisfaction	Productivity & performance
Control	Positive emotions	Morale & motivation	Attendance (sickness absence)
Balanced workload		Employee engagement	Retention (turnover)
Job security & change		Commitment	Attractiveness to recruits
Work relationships		Health	Customer/user satisfaction
Job conditions			

Source: Robertson and Flint-Taylor (2009).

Culture, however, will vary from organisation to organisation; it is something that is inherently difficult to define but you can certainly 'feel' when it is right. When immersed in an unhealthy culture it can be difficult to imagine anything different, so it's a good idea to visit other teams or organisations that have got this right.

Noteworthy, however, and as stated in the recent report 'Simplyhealth' (2012), the development of a correct culture is vitally important, but this also rests next to and alongside leadership, which is 'central to developing a culture that fosters wellbeing'. There are clearly many different types of leadership, from CEOs to senior management and then line managers, to an individual's ability to lead on a particular project. All of these types of leader, however, have clearly different responsibilities when it comes to wellbeing. However, arguably the most significant leader relationship is between employee and line manager. The line manager's role includes creating the best environment for the performance of their team members, which can be adequately addressed in the '6 essentials' framework mentioned above, whilst also providing the right balance of challenge and support. Furthermore, it is vital that leaders and managers are also equipped with the training and resources that they need to do this, and simply enough one of the most important resources is information itself, which means more access to staff and possibly staff survey findings. As a reminder, it was found in *The Sunday Times* '100 best companies to work for' that 'enlightened employers are motivating their staff by keeping them up-to-date about plans for the future' (*The Sunday Times*, 2014).

Moreover, playing a vital component in creating a strong culture during economic recessionary periods involves developing an attitude that is part of one's everyday job, so it has to be a key strand of leadership development programmes, along with effective communication skills that allow managers to interact with their teams. In essence, a strong organizational culture requires important psychological groundwork, which should entail employees being allowed to be 'open and honest' so they are not afraid to express their feelings. Hence, employers should encourage employees to give all their talents without fear and apprehension, so that creativity in such difficult times is encouraged rather than repressed. This may be achieved by an overall company ethos or through the mission statement of an organization, which needs to include short-term and long-term initiatives.

It should be remembered that culture is about 'embracing necessary change' (Simplyhealth, 2012), and change at this particular time, when economic, social and financial turbulence is taking place internationally, is more needed than ever before. Hence 'it needs to be nurtured and allowed to evolve and adapt to internal and external factors. It shouldn't be confined by a right or wrong approach, as it's not a simplistic concept or easy to define' (Simplyhealth, 2012).

In summary, therefore, it can be stated that employees today need to have the freedom of speech without the ongoing pressures of the consequences of being heard. Simultaneously, businesses need to face the reality of understanding the necessity to accommodate and support their workers in order for a healthy and productive organizational culture to permeate.

SUPPORTIVE LEADERSHIP STYLE

Leadership can be defined in a host of ways, such as:

'We must become the change we want to see': Mahatma Gandhi

'The task of a leader is to get his people from where they are to where they have not been': Henry Kissinger

'When the effective leader is finished with his work, the people say it happened naturally': Lao Tse

'Most people think of a great leader as someone who can give rousing speeches that fire up the troops. . . But to be successful in the long term, a leader must be frank with employees about the challenges as well as the opportunities they face': Bill Gates

We have selected the above quotes from a variety of internationally famous leaders throughout different times in history, and we believe that each quote offers both uniqueness and yet similarity in the definition of leadership. At the same time, the above citations sound very similar to what was recently stated in *The Sunday Times* '100 best companies to work for' (2014), where the same 'tone' is heard. Clearly, leadership is a 'phenomenon' that is distributed throughout all organizations and entities in all corners of the world. It should not be seen as a sole province of a single individual, but of the collective masses influencing one another. Thus, leadership should not be comprised of a small circle of people, or of a clique of senior staff, but it is about treating others with respect and valuing their input and contributions that they make – however small or large these may be.

It must be acknowledged from the literature (see for example, Robbins and Judge, 2009; Kassin et al., 2011) that support from the management is probably one of the strongest predictors of job satisfaction and positive psychosomatic health. Indeed, Sir Terry Leahy, previous leader at UK Tesco PLC, and 'Britain's most admired leader' from 2005 to 2010, suggests that: 'Leadership isn't about you, but rather what you can get from others: if you trust in somebody, you give them confidence to release exponential capacity. A leader will take you further than you will go on your own' (*Management Today*, cited in Weinberg and Cooper, 2012).

Similarly, and according to NICE (2009), management communication style should include 'Participation, delegation, constructive feedback, mentoring, and coaching', in addition to 'responding with sensitivity to individual emotional concerns, and symptoms of mental health problems' (NICE, 2009, cited in Weinberg and Cooper, 2012).

Unfortunately in recent years – and probably as a consequence of the difficult economic times – the managerial styles used in organizations to lead people have clearly not been satisfactory. Indeed as Worrall and Cooper (2012) discovered in their groundbreaking research, it appears that 'an abrasive managerial style' is more evident, which as we have discussed in this book is clearly more problematic. Thus, from the above, and in summary, we can certainly suggest that during unstable and fragile economic times good leadership skills are of paramount importance in the wellbeing of employees and for a healthy and prosperous organization to develop. It is vital that managers strive, and simultaneously that harmonious working relationships flourish as both managers and the workforce, from shop floor to top floor, aim to understand each other. One needs to remember and acknowledge that everybody has a different working approach, with their unique personal demands, and it is therefore inappropriate and naïve to attempt to treat everybody in the same way.

As the literature on diversity suggests (see for example Crisp, 2010; Van Knippenberg, 2010, cited in Crisp, 2010), a diverse workforce is greatly advantageous during this global recession, and some scientists believe that a diverse workforce gives the additional benefit in allowing companies to succeed. Therefore it is advised that people should aim to develop and inspire each other, which in return should provide the basis for a beneficial and innovative working team.

Indeed, in *The Sunday Times* '100 best companies' survey, repeated themes such as 'striving towards common goals' and 'warm hearts bring cheer and rewards' are issues that are topping the working environment. Therefore, in today's turbulent economic climate, one should aim to foster a correct balance of positive behaviour and simultaneously enhance cooperation and collaboration amongst colleagues. According to Simplyhealth (2012), the following strategies have recently been proposed to demonstrate ways that a leadership programme can identify key changes that need to be implemented. These can be business strategies or indeed psychological factors, and below are several ways to put this into practice:

1. Senior managers to visit the shop floor: a divide can often form between the senior staff and the lower-level employees of an organization. As leaders are engaged at all levels it is important for top-level management to engage with all employees.
2. Encourage learning through internal and external training programmes: there is a wealth of information online that employees can access to aid their development. The important thing is to notice that this forms part of their day job and they therefore should be encouraged to access it. People can also draw upon the knowledge that they already have. Internal training courses are inexpensive and effective as you are harnessing the knowledge of your staff and sharing information. Mentoring sessions are also a great way for people to learn from others and to develop strengths in areas where they may have weaknesses.
3. Use the communication tools at your disposal: communicate regularly to your staff through different media. Employees like to be communicated to in different ways, so it is important to use a variety of methods including email, staff intranet and internal newsletters or magazines.
4. Staff update sessions: once a month, get together as an organization and share your business performance with your staff. You can make these sessions more personable by introducing staff awards.
5. Staff forums or a staff consultative committee: this is an opportunity once a month for representatives of departments to get together

and discuss staff issues, which can be raised anonymously and in confidence.

6. Focus groups: an ideal way to get your leadership objectively on the table and to discuss with employees at all levels. These should be as open and honest as possible and the results should be shared with staff in a timely manner to show that they are shaping the decision making process.

7. Engagement surveys: these are a good way to understand how employees are feeling, and are excellent benchmarks to improve the level of engagement and the psychological wellbeing of your staff. They can be repeated periodically to gauge results and so you can formulate an action plan to address any issues highlighted.

COPING WITH PSYCHOLOGICAL STRAIN IN THE JOB

Until now, emphasis has been put on possible stress prevention in the workplace. However, this chapter would not be complete if possible solutions to symptoms of strain were not addressed. In 1851, John Ruskin, the social reformer at the beginning of the Industrial Revolution suggested: 'In order that people may be happy in their work, these three things are needed: they must be fit for it, they must not do too much of it, and they must have a sense of success in it'.

Certainly then, and as stated by Cooper (2013): 'The irony of the great banking crash of 2008 is that from the ashes of the recession has emerged the happiness or wellbeing movement'. To that end, the World Economic Forum now has as one of its Global Agenda Councils 'Wellbeing and Mental Health', and the International Congress of Applied Psychology (ICAP) held in Paris in July 2014 had as its slogan 'From Sustainability to Wellbeing'. With this prevailing economic downturn and globalization being recognized and felt internationally (see parts I and II of this book), this has given the majority of us time to absorb information, think and reflect, and hopefully move forward to achieve a healthy balance to our overall wellbeing. If this is the case, we are eventually and slowly taking a 360-degree turn, to readdress health and happiness issues in the working environment. Therefore, it seems more advantageous to adopt a multi-faceted strategy, whereby structural organizational changes are addressed, and also stress that symptoms can be treated very quickly. Therefore and not surprisingly, organizational psychologists tend to tackle psychological and emotional strain in the workplace by utilizing 'stress management techniques' to identify symptoms of strain and methods to help the individual worker to deal with them. Such recommendations include assertiveness training programmes, increased and better communication skills, and relaxation techniques. Furthermore, in today's problematic economic climate an increase and greater usage of job-seeking techniques and interview skills may certainly help the individual to cope more effectively. However, in order to best deal with psychological symptoms of strain at work, one necessary yet fundamental step is needed and that is: raise awareness of symptoms. This may seem very simple – and yet it is very rarely taken into consideration and few companies appear to play by this rule. Awareness can be made via in-house seminars, workshops and even simple websites and internet messages can act as a basic teaching aid to manage stress in the job. By flagging up the correct messages effective coping strategies can then be utilized, ranging from shop floor to top floor needs.

In the working environment, strategies for effective coping are usually work based; however, in the forthcoming and final chapter individual and outside stress management techniques are offered for the reader's perusal. Indeed it is believed that both organizational effectiveness and individual wellness techniques need to be combined to have full effectiveness in combating the levels of stress experienced by the individual, family and organization.

Without going into great detail here (further elaboration is given in the forthcoming chapter), popular stress management techniques follow the cognitive-behavioural approach (Greenberg, 1996; Giga et al., 2003). In this type of therapy emphasis is placed on relaxation techniques that aim at lowering psychological arousal levels in addition to changing our cognitive strategies to be more proactive. Often, clinical psychologists prefer to use more than one approach, and this will depend on both the interaction with the person and the situation so that the therapy can be aimed to achieve better results. We would like to emphasize at this point, however, that all stress management techniques focus on enhancing individuals' awareness, stamina, and ability to confront and cope with occupational stress in these difficult economic times.

RELAXATION TECHNIQUES: GENERAL APPLICATIONS

As mentioned above, there are many relaxation techniques (readers wishing to obtain greater detail may refer to meditation techniques, autogenic training, progressive relaxation techniques, biofeedback, and yoga which are some simple examples; see, for instance, Greenberg, 1996).

However, what needs to be conveyed is that all relaxation techniques should be 'part and parcel' of a comprehensive stress management programme, and should relate to the level of emotional arousal and serve as both direct and indirect interventions between stress, disease and illness (Greenberg, 1996). As stated in Weinberg and Cooper (2012), meditation has been modified from transcendental techniques, which are used in employment settings primarily because they can be learned easily and are quickly applied to the work settings where they can reduce physiological and emotional symptoms (Murphy, 1996). Alternatively, one can apply cognitive-behavioural methods which primarily target people's cognitive thinking strategies. This technique has been widely used on a number of different occupational types, ranging from police officers to nurses and teachers (Freedy and Hobfall, 1994, cited in Weinberg and Cooper, 2012). Finally, the popular RET therapy (Rational Emotional Therapy) (Albert Ellis, 1977) attempts to stop the individual from having negative and often irrational aspects of thinking. Primarily, RET therapy aims at replacing irrational thoughts with rational and positive cognitions. For example, and as cited in Weinberg and Cooper (2012), one could start by tracing the individual's appraisal of threat in a situation, for example 'redundancies are likely to occur', to the worries that have given rise to it, such as 'it might be my job', which can help to identify emotional and behavioural consequences such as 'I am so upset I will stop putting effort into my work'. Rejecting the irrational aspects of these beliefs, for example 'doing something which gets me a disciplinary hearing will not help my job prospects here or elsewhere', can help to restructure the person's outlook in a positive way: 'I will keep working hard to ensure I get a good reference and also make sure I have got my eye on new job opportunities'. According to Murphy (1996), well-designed programmes can lead to improved overall wellbeing and it has been proven to show a reduction in psychological distress such as blood pressure levels, heart rate and stress hormone levels. However, there is little evidence to suggest that these changes will continue in the longer term unless skills are updated periodically – and we suggest that this should be done even more frequently than in the past, to coincide with the vast changes and adaptations that are taking place in the economy. This way, using correct stress management programmes as part of an overall strategy to which the organization is committed, is most likely to be effective in reducing psychological strain in the workforce.

It can be concluded, however, that the majority of the literature assessing stress management programmes has provided mixed results. Nonetheless, many studies have shown positive outcomes, for instance in reducing burnout among nurses (Ewers et al., 2002) and in improving work performance among doctors (Michie and Sandu, 1994, cited in

Weinberg and Cooper, 2012). In addition, the latter produced the interesting, yet unexpected emphasis on the 'opportunity to discuss their problems and collective support', which was similar to the confirmed results in the doctoral thesis findings (Fotinatos, 1996), showing the vital importance of social support networks in the job. This again underlines the importance of social support in the work environment for all types of people, whereby employees in public and private sectors, blue collar and white collar workers, need the emotional support of colleagues at work.

COPING WITH SYMPTOMS OF STRAIN IN THE JOB

Workplace health programmes have achieved increasing popularity in organizations in recent years and this trend has primarily taken place in North America, where they aim to promote 'vigorous cardiovascular exercise, activities which promote muscle tone and flexibility, lifestyle counseling and fun and fellowship' (Dishman, 1988, cited in Weinberg and Cooper, 2012). The aim of such programmes is to target a reduction of the costs incurred from employee illness while improving productivity and maintaining good health. Although evaluation has been less than systematic during the past years, benefits have been found for both the physical and mental health of the employee, as well as the functioning of the organization (Voit, 2001). An employee fitness programme at the ING Bank in the Netherlands resulted in significantly reduced absenteeism for both regular and occasional participants (Kerr and Vos, 1993, cited in Weinberg and Cooper, 2012), while a study of automotive plants in Michigan established the cost effectiveness and benefits of employee health and fitness schemes, which provided both exercise options and follow-up counselling. Nestlé's commitment to the World Health Organization guidelines saw it launch a 'Global Corporate Challenge' to encourage its staff to walk at least 10,000 steps each day. Their head of employee wellness, Dr David Batman, recognized that 'during the recession a lot of businesses are cutting back on these programs and people are worried about leaving the office, but we need these schemes more than ever'.

The combination of a growing proportion of sedentary jobs and the increase in stressors related to job insecurity presents its own risks to employee wellbeing in these difficult economic times. Estimates of increased chances of heart disease through a sedentary lifestyle vary, but its occurrence is almost twice as high in the inactive compared to active individuals. 'It is a well known fact, that physical inactivity represents a risk factor for coronary heart disease (CHD), along with the well-known problems caused by high blood pressure, high cholesterol levels and smoking' (US Department of Health and Human Services, 1996, cited in Weinberg and Cooper, 2012).

In addition, the incidence of coronary heart disease appears to be directly related to the way people handle stress at work. A third of the effects of job stress on CHD among employees are due to its effect on health behaviours and stress chemical pathways. A London-based study of 10,308 civil servants confirmed the link between work stress and metabolic syndrome, which is characterized by three of the following: elevated blood pressure; high density lipoprotein cholesterol; glucose after fasting; triglycerides; and abdominal obesity. Those exposed to chronic work strain (on more than three occasions) had more than double the chances of developing metabolic syndrome than those who had not (Chandola et al., 2006, cited in Weinberg and Cooper, 2012). Taking the usual risk factors into account, job insecurity, along with work pressure and the individual's 'need for control', was shown to predict coronary heart disease in a study of 416 middle-aged blue-collar workers over a six-year period (Siegrist et al., 1990). The positive news is that changes in behaviour can alter outcomes for the individual (Anderson, 2004). In fact Australian economists projected that half an hour's daily walking for five to seven days each week by those able to do so, could lead to healthcare savings of AUS$ 126.73 million (Zheng et al., 2009).

INDIVIDUAL COPING STRATEGIES IN THE WORKPLACE

In recent years, it has been acknowledged by the majority of the working population that our psychological health is equally as important as our physical health, and therefore in these difficult and challenging times, emotional stress is a far bigger problem than in the past. The feelings of stress and anxiety that exist in the workplace amongst people who are facing uncertainty and job losses is quite understandable, as is the sense of learned helplessness and negativity linked to potentially depressing situations. These emotional feelings can result in poor psychological health that can spill over into various aspects of the way we work. For example, the individual may be prone to sick leave, or as we have discussed throughout this book, contribute to an increase in presenteeism at work, and such accumulating problems take their toll on all organizations. However, it is doubtless the organization that has full duty of care and responsibility for its employees.

At the time of the Great Depression of the 1930s, Western Electric Company in the United States recognized the value of 'paying more attention to feelings and concerns' of workers (Lee and Gray, 1994, p. 218, cited in Weinberg and Cooper, 2012). As part of the company's research into productivity, interviews with 20,000 employees highlighted the relationship between the opportunity to express emotion at work and improved functioning as well as a decrease in tension. Since the 1970s there has been steady growth in similar initiatives. The most common is the Employee Assistance Programmes (EAP), which provide counselling for individuals, and often their families too, regarding both work-related and non-work problems, including relationship difficulties, illness worries, redundancy or retirement concerns, and financial worries. It is the case that these problems are elevated during these difficult times, and so these factors need to be addressed rapidly and efficiently, more so than ever in the past. Correct application of EAPs, which are defined as 'The provision of brief psychological therapy for employees of an organisation, which is paid for by the employer' (McLeod and Henderson, 2003, cited in Weinberg and Cooper, 2012) will undoubtedly provide a safety net to individuals and families in these vulnerable times, to assist in ensuring better physical and psychological functioning at work.

REFERENCES

Andersen, L.B. (2004). Relative risk of mortality in the physically inactive is underestimated because of real changes in exposure level during follow-up. *American Journal of Epidemiology*, 160, 189–95.

Bradon, P. (2009). The best companies to work for, available at: www.http//business.timesonline.co.uk.

Cartwright, S. and Cooper, C.L. (2011). *Oxford Handbook of Organizational Wellbeing*. Oxford: Oxford University Press, pp. 109–32.

Cooper, C.L. (2012). *Health and Safety Practitioner*: The Happiness @ Work Agenda.

Cooper, C.L. (2013). 'UK has a cultural problem of "overworking"', says HR thinker Cary Cooper, *HR Magazine*, 16 May. Available at: http://www.hrmagazine.co.uk.

Crisp, R. (2010). *The Psychology of Social and Cultural Diversity*. Chichester: Wiley-Blackwell.

Dewe, P.J. and Kompier, M. (2008). *Foresight Mental Capital and Well-Being Project: Well-being and work: Future Challenges*. London: The Government Office for Science.

Dewe, P.J., O'Driscoll, M.P. and Cooper, C.L. (2010). *Coping with Work Stress: A Review and Critique*. Chichester: Wiley-Blackwell.

Ellis, A. (1977). The basic clinical theory of rational-emotive therapy. In A. Ellis and R. Grieger (eds), *Handbook of Rational-Emotive Therapy*, New York: Springer-Verlag.

Ewers, P., Bradshaw, T., McGovern, J. and Ewers, B. (2002). Does training in psychosocial interventions reduce burnout rates in forensic nurses? *Journal of Advanced Nursing*, 37, 470–76.

Fotinatos, R.S.J. (1996). Doctoral thesis, *A Community Wide Survey of Occupational Stress*. Manchester: UMIST.

Fotinatos-Ventouratos, R.S.J. and Cooper, C.L. (1998). Social class differences and occupational stress. *International Journal of Stress Management*, 5 (4), 211–22.

Giga, S.I., Cooper, C.L. and Faragher, B. (2003). The development of a framework for a comprehensive approach to stress management interventions at work. *International Journal of Stress Management*, 10, 280–96.

Government Office for Science (2008). Mental capital and wellbeing: Making the most of ourselves in the 21st Century, UK Government Foresight Project, London: The Government Office for Science.

Greenberg, J.S. (1996). *Comprehensive Stress Management*. 5th edn, New York: McGraw-Hill.

Health and Safety Executive (HSE) (2009). Stress-related and psychological disorders: Summary, available at: www.hse.gov.uk/statistics/causedis/stress/index.htm.

Kassin, S., Fein, S. and Markus, H.R. (2011). *Social Psychology*. 8th edn, Belmont, CA: Wadsworth Cengage Learning.

Leka, S., Griffiths, A. and Cox, T. (2007). Work organization and stress, in Protecting Workers' Health Series, No. 3, Nottingham: Institute of Work, Health and Organisations.

Murphy, L.R. (1996). Stress management techniques: Secondary prevention of stress. In M.J. Schabracq, J.A.M. Winnubst and C.L. Cooper (eds), *Handbook of Work and Health Psychology*. Chichester: John Wiley and Sons, pp. 427–41.

National Institute for Health and Clinical Excellence (NICE) (2009). *Public Health Guidance 22, Promoting Mental Wellbeing through Productive and Healthy Working Conditions: Guidance for Employers*. London: NICE.

Robbins, S.P. and Judge, T.A. (2009). *Organizational Behaviour*. 13th edn, Upper Saddle River, NJ: Pearson Prentice Hall.

Robertson, I. and Cooper, C.L. (2011). *Wellbeing: Productivity and Happiness at Work*. Basingstoke: Palgrave Macmillan.

Robertson, I.T. and Flint-Taylor, J. (2009). Leadership, psychological well-being and organizational outcomes. In Cartwright, S. and Cooper, C.L. (eds), *Oxford Handbook on Organisational Well-being*, Oxford: Oxford University Press, pp. 159–79.

Sainsbury Centre for Mental Health (2007). Mental health at work: Developing the business case. Policy Paper no. 8. London: Sainsbury Centre for Mental Health.

Siegrist, J., Peter, R., Jung, A., Cremer, P. and Seidel, D. (1990). Low status control, high effort at work and ischaemic heart disease: Prospective evidence from blue collar men. *Social Science and Medicine*, 31, 1127–34.

Simplyhealth (2012). Simplyhealth: We can bothered, available at: www.simply-health.co.uk.

The Sunday Times (2014). *The Sunday Times* 100 best companies to work for, available at: http://features.thesundaytimes.co.uk/public/best100companies/live/template, accessed 14 January 2014.

Van Knippenberg, D. (2003). Intergroup relations in organizations. In M. West,

D. Tjosvold and K.G. Smith (eds), *International Handbook of Organizational Teamwork and Cooperative Working*, Chichester: Wiley, pp. 381–99.

Voit, S. (2001). Work-site health and fitness programs: Impact on the employee and employer. *Work*, 16, 273–86.

Weinberg, A. and Cooper, C.L. (2012). *Stress in Turbulent Times*. Basingstoke: Palgrave Macmillan.

Worrall, L. and Cooper, C.L. (2006). *The Quality of Working Life 2006*. London: Chartered Management Institute (CMI).

Worrall, L. and Cooper, C.L. (2012). *The Quality of Working Life 2012: Managers' Wellbeing, Motivation and Productivity*. London: Chartered Management Institute (CMI).

Zheng, H., Ehrlich, F. and Amin, J. (2009). Economic evaluation of the direct healthcare cost savings resulting from the use of walking interventions to prevent coronary heart disease in Australia. *International Journal of Health Care Finance and Economics*, 10 (2), 187–201.

8. Individual and societal wellbeing: an agenda for the future: post economic crisis

INTRODUCTION

In the previous chapter we provided an overview of critical issues pertaining to organizational effectiveness and wellbeing at work. Our specific intention was not to describe or evaluate particular types of stress intervention techniques or programmes in detail, but rather we emphasized underlying issues that we believe are of paramount importance during this ongoing recessionary period. This book, however, would not be complete if we did not highlight individual coping strategies that can be utilized in societies that have been severely tarnished by this economic crisis. Indeed, and as we have shown throughout this book, organizational, societal and individual wellbeing go together and all parties therefore must take equal and full responsibility for prosperity to emerge and for post-recessionary periods to commence. Furthermore, it is believed that all types of stress management initiatives are a *shared* entity and therefore no particular party can take sole responsibility for the given stressors of our times.

For the individual, however, coping involves many steps and procedures, although by and large we are referring to the *emotional* and *practical* solutions that can be utilized. Simultaneously, we acknowledge that everybody is unique and so one particular strategy may not be applicable to all – in reality, therefore, what we suggest below may work for some but not for others, or may be applicable in one culture and society and not in another. Nonetheless, we believe that even partial attempts and applications to cope are better than no remedy at all, as all types of safety nets act as a buffer to stress.

DEFINITION OF COPING

Starting with a definition of coping, one may suggest, therefore, that coping is a 'shifting process' – in other words, moving away from the stress-related problem – in some shape and form. The 'shifting process' was first described by Lazarus and Folkman in 1984, and these two scientists emphasized that all individuals will respond to change in different ways and at different times in their life. Thus in our current economically difficult and unstable times we must seek to move away from the stressor and make the most of any positive opportunities that are appealing to us. Basically, then, we are suggesting that there are positive and negative ways of coping which can be translated into healthy versus unhealthy coping.

POSITIVE VERSUS NEGATIVE WAYS OF COPING

Negative ways of coping imply unproductive and unhealthy ways of dealing with the stressor. These stressors can be either acute or chronic, yet the fundamental issue at stake is whether the individual is responding in a healthy and adaptive manner. For instance, responding to an already aggressive colleague at work in a similarly confrontational manner is both unhealthy for the individual and also unproductive: to put it simply, it will get you nowhere! In the short term, the venting of such negative emotions may provide the individual with a temporary feeling of satisfaction, although in the long term the individual will not benefit from acting in such a negative way: two wrongs will not make a right! Thus, however unhappy an individual may become in the workplace, coping in the first instance by giving vent to their emotions may not be advantageous in the long term. What one therefore needs to find is an 'acceptable expression of such uncomfortable experiences in a manner which does not cause distress to ourselves, or others' (Dewe et al., 2010).

At the present time, many people are looking at the future full of doubt, scepticism and fear, yet we all deserve a new start and fresh opportunity to hope. In essence, we need to 'restart our engines', with a long process of emotional and psychological rebuilding so that we can be better equipped to benefit from and also accept outside help. More specifically, therefore, we emphasize that individuals need to cope with stress effectively and tackle wellbeing in a step-like and systematic manner.

At the beginning of this book, and primarily in Part II, we described to the reader a wide range of psychological resources which form the foundations for ability to cope with challenges. For example, we have discussed the concept of control in the job, and the interaction between the individual and organization on a variety of issues, such as the psychological contract, which we now know is the phenomenon of the unwritten expectations which guide us in our job. Furthermore, today we are slowly getting accustomed to the fact that we need to 'cut our cloth to suit our circumstances'. Understandably, however, we also acknowledge that this may not be an easy process, and indeed this may take time and, simultaneously, it may challenge our internal resources and put pressure on the individual, family and society as a whole. However, as Palmer and Cooper suggested in the early stages of economic difficulty, one good way to cope is to be sure and positive about your own abilities (Palmer and Cooper, 2010). In other words, one needs to value and respect the self.

VALUING AND RESPECTING YOURSELF

One of the most serious causes of neglect is when one loses respect for the self and no longer values oneself. This feeling is often exacerbated in difficult times like today, with issues such as losing one's job and facing immense difficulties in an uncertain economic climate. Whilst it is very easy to devalue yourself, it is exactly at these moments in life that one needs to engage in positive thinking and to remember that job loss, for example, is not about the individual and loss of skills, rather it reflects the position of an organization and whole global economy. Moreover, feelings of injustice and unfairness in times of uncertainty are natural and clearly understandable, yet looking at the situation in an unemotional manner and objectively is preferable and we would understand these emotions if others were facing similar situations. Hence a position of 'stand back', 'detach' and 'reflect' is necessary, and the circumstances due to globalization and world recession are not about the individual's ability per se, but rather about the factual situation brought about by world economic turmoil. In summary, therefore, it is totally wrong to personally attribute job loss and economic difficulties to one's own defeat and actions, and one should remember that in some financially starved countries, youth unemployment has exceeded 60 per cent at the time of writing this book (Greece, for example; see Eurostat figures, January, 2014). In other words, one needs to put into perspective the potential negatives and become fully engaged both emotionally and practically in what is going on. This can be done if we acknowledge, record and periodically update 'our knowledge, skills and abilities' (KSAs) and, rather than wait for an unfortunate event to occur, we should be more proactive in what we do, prioritize our needs and itemize job tasks. In this way, we create a more solid vision of what we are currently doing, which can result in our being accurate in what we actually contribute both within and outside the organization. Table 8.1 is a self-appraisal exercise of knowledge, skills and abilities (adopted from Weinberg et al., 2010).

As we can see from Table 8.1, this is a self-appraisal exercise, and

Table 8.1   Reflecting and making explicit the skills we take for granted

As part of my daily routine, I. . .	Strongly agree	Agree	Disagree	Strongly Disagree
Communicate with others in person or by phone/email				
Seek to advise others on how to best solve their problems				
Work well as part of a team				
Enjoy socializing with others				
Am interested in learning new skills				
Am concerned about how I interact with others				
Want to try my best at all tasks				
Like to make a positive difference				
Have specialized knowledge, skills and abilities in my area of expertise				
Take initiative in organizing events at work				

we should acknowledge that carrying out such self-reflection tasks is not only valuable during difficult periods, but should be viewed as part and parcel of any individual's coping strategy regime, and therefore conducted periodically. In other words, as the British Girl Guides motto states, 'be prepared'. In this instance, therefore, in addition to regularly updating our curriculum vitae, we need to make our skills explicit and not take them for granted, and by having all our tools ready and sharpened, this gives us all a valuable head-start if things are about to change.

Moreover, and in addition to being fully prepared with an updated curriculum vitae, there is also a need for people seeking employment to regularly attend workshops and seminars to emphasize the value of their interpersonal skills and interview techniques. In these difficult financial times, one notes that many of these workshops and seminars are also being offered at a reduced cost, and in some instances no fee is charged for the unemployed. Taking advantage of such programmes is not only beneficial, but allows the individual to further their skills and to be up-to-date with various initiatives. Furthermore, in times of economic and severe financial cutbacks, individuals may wish to offer their own skills through voluntary activities, as it appears that many sectors have had huge cutbacks. Each person therefore needs to be fully fledged in utilizing their skills in both work and non-work contexts.

THE NEED FOR AUTONOMY

Throughout this book, and consistent with earlier findings (Fotinatos, 1996; Fotinatos-Ventouratos and Cooper, 1998), there is a great need for all individuals, irrespective of their background, gender, age or occupation, to feel in control of events and situations. Human beings have an immense need to retain their self-esteem and this is often achieved by having feelings of control over events and situations. Literally taken from the Latin word *aestimare* (to estimate), each one of us needs to have a high estimation of what we can do, and a vital component of this estimation is to feel that we have control and autonomy in various aspects of our lives. It is the 'I can do this' feeling that is needed, and it serves to demonstrate to the self and others that we are proactive in wanting to make something happen. We believe it is this spirit that will assist all of us in difficult and challenging times, and certainly it helps us to build up our resilience and our cognitive and emotion-focused approach for improved wellbeing in the organization and society at large.

For the purpose of our self-esteem, it is not the activity per se that is of importance, but the positive feelings that we can generate by doing certain tasks. It is the psychological feeling that 'we are in control' that is vitally important for our psychological wellbeing. Thus the activity can be as simple as running an errand for someone else or doing a form of physical exercise, which will make the positive difference and serve as a valuable signpost to the individual that we are proactive in wanting to make things happen, that ultimately we have autonomy, and furthermore, that we are the ones determining the events rather than being on the receiving end of what the world has in store (Siegrist, 2009). This may simply be reflected in the language we use to describe events around us and the connotation it gives. For instance, two different meanings can be generated from the wording of 'I will try and do my best', in comparison to 'I do not think that I will be able to do my best'. Each of these statements, whether applied at home or in the work domain, carry different meanings of responsibility and accountability of what we are doing and also how we are performing tasks, and simultaneously we send out clear cut communication channels about how we view ourselves and influence events around us. By showing a willingness and determination to complete tasks then serves as an indication to the self and others in terms of certainty and autonomy.

BUILDING RESILIENCE, RESISTANCE AND STAMINA

In seeking to understand why some people cope better than others, one needs to focus on the issues of building resilience, resistance and stamina. Resilience can indeed be studied from various angles, such as in times of bereavement, difficulty in coping with life in general, but also in crisis times – just like the current economic crisis being experienced in most corners of the globe. Here we can see that some people cope better than others, and according to many psychologists, it is exactly this resilience, rather than collapse and recovery, that is the most common and healthy outcome from all types of traumatic events. In fact there are many scientific definitions that have been provided to describe personal resilience, some of which are stated below in Box 8.1.

As can be seen from Box 8.1 there is a multiplicity of definitions, all of which provide different and added value according to the individual and situation at hand. However, we think that a generic way of defining resilience is more applicable during turbulent economic times, and therefore we suggest a simple definition of resilience such as 'the individual's ability to bounce back from adversity to equilibrium'.

In this case, the adversity is the economic crisis, and to effectively 'bounce back' to a desired state of equilibrium, several personality factors need to be taken into consideration. For example *mental toughness* is needed, whereby in one study, mental toughness was found to be related to optimism and the ability to cope with pressure, and specifically with a tendency to tackle issues and problems directly rather than using avoidance to cope (cited in Cooper et al., 2013). Furthermore, it is suggested that applying *intelligence and problem-solving initiatives* is beneficial. That is, people with good 'problem-solving' abilities may still feel anxious and stressed at times, but they have a better chance of figuring out a solution: their intellectual ability acts as a protective factor against stress and poor performance. This does not mean, however, that the most resilient people are those with the highest levels of intelligence! It is more a question of being able to develop a sound understanding of your situation, and to evaluate how it is likely to develop and what options are open to you. Finally, *psychological hardiness* is another personality characteristic that has been proven to be related to resilience (Kobasa, 1979). More

---

BOX 8.1   DEFINITIONS AND DESCRIPTIONS OF PERSONAL RESILIENCE

'Resilience is best defined as an outcome of successful adaptation to adversity. Characteristics of the person and situation may identify resilient processes, but only if they lead to healthier outcomes following stressful circumstances.' (Zautra and others, p.4)

'Resilience has numerous meanings in prior research, but generally refers to a pattern of functioning indicative of "positive adaptation" in the context of "risk" or adversity.' (Ong and others p.82)

'Resilience is a term psychologists use to refer to people's ability to cope with and find meaning in. . . .stressful life events, in which individuals must respond with healthy intellectual functioning and supportive social relationships (Richardson, 2002).' (Mayer and Faber, p.95)

'Resilience refers to individual differences or life experiences that help people to cope positively with adversity, make them better able to deal with stress in the future, and confer protection from the development of mental disorders under stress (Richardson, 2002).' (Skodol p.113)

'Resilience is a broad concept that generally refers to positive adaptation in any kind of dynamic system that comes under challenge or threat.' (Masten and Obradovic, 2008)

'Human resilience refers to the processes or pattern of positive adaptation and development in the context of significant threats to an individual's life or function.' (Masten and Wright, p.215)

Source: Taken from Cooper et al. (2013).

---

specifically, in the original research by Susan Kobasa, her study involved comparing a group of managers and executives who suffered ill-health due to stress with a second group who remained healthy under similar pressures. Those who remained healthy under pressure were found to have higher levels of the '3Cs': the dispositions of Commitment, Control and Challenge. *Commitment* refers to engaging with one's environment and having a sense of purpose or meaning. *Control* refers to feeling able to influence events (sometimes described as an internal locus of control). *Challenge* refers to seeing change as normal and welcome – an opportunity rather than a threat. Interestingly, however, in more recent research (see for example Cooper et al., 2013) the '3Cs' are presented as 'resilient attitudes' rather than dispositions, and are seen as being complemented by 'two vital skills', of transformational coping (transforming potentially stressful changes to your advantage) and social support (interacting with others in a constructive way that builds and preserves relationships). Thus, however one may view resilience, it is suggested that it is a vital component in assisting each and every one of us in regulating the stress–strain relationship, which is evident and acute in our current times.

THE PSYCHOLOGICAL CONTRACT: REVIEWED AND REVISED

Periodically throughout this book, we have discussed the term and implications of the psychological contract (Rosseau, 1989; 1995). It may be feasible to suggest that in difficult and challenging economic times, the psychological contract that we once created may be subject to change. Basically, changing times means changing expectations – and hopefully these expectations will be realistic expectations that each person can meet. For instance, the advent of job loss or job insecurity encourages us to question the priority we have given to a particular organization or type of work. For example, working today in paid employment means the transactions between employer and employee are likely to be altered – for instance, previously self-statements such as 'why should I be so concerned about this job?' may result in renegotiating this contract within ourselves, and assessing its importance. Moreover, starting over again and seeking new employment means we should re-evaluate our needs, concerns and simultaneously assess our knowledge, skills and abilities – as discussed above (see Table 8.1). Taking, then, our knowledge, abilities and skills as a coherent whole, we can apply our beliefs and rewrite the psychological contract in relation to looking for work. For example:

- My knowledge, abilities and skills are broad enough to apply in the working environment.
- There are many tasks that I can excel in, and others frequently report that I am good at.
- By showing others what I can do, will increase the chance of being successful.
- Things at the present time may not seem fair and just, yet all circumstances are likely to change.
- Past employers have an insight into my track record and so they may be worth approaching for a reference letter.
- I have gained employment in the past and therefore I will again.
- My support system is plentiful – with friends, acquaintances and family offering me help, if needed.
- Believing and trusting myself will allow others to believe in me too – and as the famous saying goes 'if you do not love yourself, you cannot expect others to love you'.

- I am in control of my situation.
- It costs nothing to try and ask.

The above ten bullet points serve not only as a valuable exit strategy, but we also make a contract with ourselves that we are as indispensable as possible. Here then, we remove the doubts and close the gap between what we want (a) and how things should be fairer and more just (b). By minimizing the gap between a + b, we rebalance the psychological contract. In summary, therefore, we can rewrite the psychological contract and obtain quite an accurate picture of what we can expect in terms of finances, expectations of home and work, as well as relationship dynamics in difficult times.

In the final section below, however, the authors suggest that it is necessary to be aware, manage and act upon how we feel and think – and also how others feel and think about us. To put it simply, one needs to be fully aware of the 'looking glass self', a term originally coined by the famous sociologist Cooley (1902, cited in Kassin et al., 2011) to describe the essential need to be accurately aware of how individuals and others see us.

PHYSICAL WELLBEING AND THE NEED FOR COPING IN POST ECONOMIC CRISIS TIMES

Some years ago in my doctoral thesis, which was supervised by Professor Sir Cary Cooper, we became quite alarmed by the answers given to a simple question that was posed in my research to approximately 2,500 people representing all socio-economic groups. The question was 'Do you take a form of physical exercise?' and if so, 'always, sometimes, occasionally or never'? To our surprise on running this simple statistic we found that people who exercised on a regular basis (defined as once or twice per week), were significantly more likely to show better physical and psychological health ($p < .0001$). Although this may sound a 'simple remedy', and almost like a cliché, the fundamental need to take some form of exercise is vitally important for our wellbeing and cannot be underestimated. We emphasize to readers, however, that it does not have to be constant visits to the gym, but in these stressful times physical exercise of all sorts – a brisk walk, jogging, swimming, tennis – are long recognized ways to promote health and wellbeing. Indeed in the university that I work for (The American College of Greece, Athens), keep fit classes have been initiated for all lecturers, staff and administrators, which take place in the so-called 'activity hour', when no lectures are scheduled. This is an ideal opportunity not only to exercise and take a break from the 9 to 5 desk work and teaching, but it is also to increase social relationships and have fun in such difficult times. The link between psychological strain and physical wellbeing has been long recognized, and so elevated levels of blood pressure, increase in blood chemicals linked with poorer health (for example, high-density lipoprotein cholesterol) and abdominal obesity are known responses to chronic exposure to stress and work. Indeed, Lundberg and Cooper (2011), in their book *The Science of Occupational Health*, clearly state that 'Physical activity includes all movements of the body produced by skeletal muscles which use energy. . .The importance of physical exercise for stress tolerance has been documented in several studies' (p. 118). Indeed, regular walking for 30 minutes a day seems to be sufficient to achieve positive effects (Lee et al., 2000, cited in Lundberg and Cooper, 2011), and physical activity has been found to reduce depressive symptoms (Penninx et al., 2002, cited in Lundberg and Cooper, 2011), to reduce insulin resistance in overweight individuals (Tuomilehto et al., 2001), and to have beneficial effects on fibromyalgia patients (Richards and Scott, 2002, cited in Lundberg and Cooper, 2011).

Such findings therefore strongly support the need for us to consider strategies which might benefit our physical health. There is indeed a lot that both organizations can do and promote, as well as what local communities can offer, and what the individual can also do for the benefit of their health. For example, Yu et al. (2003) found out that middle-aged men with no previous history of coronary heart disease, who adopted intensive leisure activities and took up physical activity such as jogging, swimming and taking the stairs rather than the elevator, significantly reduced their risks of mortality. Fitting exercise into our everyday life and scheduling it in our agenda will certainly improve healthy behaviour and promote a healthier, sharpened mind.

RELAXATION TIME

During this economic crisis period, when stress levels are elevated, the opportunity to relax seems to fade, and yet it is at such difficult and challenging moments of our lives that we all need time to relax, clear our minds and wind down! However, the simple qualities of everyday life often become a shadow that fails to materialize, and yet these simplicities are for many a vital safety net. Relaxation time does not have to be a grandiose event – what we advocate are the enjoyable and simple moments of life that we should indulge in, for example, taking a walk, smelling the roses, listening to music, going to the sea and socializing with friends – all of these things can be enjoyed and should not suffer.

Additionally, and as discussed in Chapter 7, there are a variety of relaxation techniques that one could recommend which are primarily designed to reduce physiological arousal, which tends to become greater when exposed to stressors. If implemented well, they are known to induce feelings of calm and help bring down our physiological and psychological state to an equilibrium. The outcome therefore, is to reduce tension and anxiety and to provide a greater sense of wellbeing and control. At a physical level, relaxation can keep blood pressure in check, reduce muscle tension, lower cholesterol in the bloodstream and improve clarity of thinking (Weinberg et al., 2010). Progressive muscle relaxation utilizes the alternate tensing and relaxation of muscle groups, for example, hands, shoulders, legs and so forth, whereas meditation focuses on the mind, in an attempt to clear one's thoughts. Biofeedback, alternatively, has been defined as 'the use of instrumentation to mirror psychophysiological processes of which the individual is not normally aware and which may be brought under voluntary control' (Greenberg, 2008). Really, this is just a way of saying that biofeedback is receiving information about what is occurring in your body at a particular time and then helping you to control that occurrence. Consequently, a basal body thermometer can be considered a biofeedback instrument – albeit slow and not as accurate as more sophisticated equipment since it gives you information about a parameter of the body (its core temperature). Biofeedback has many benefits, not least of which is the demonstration (objectively and physiologically) that we have much greater control of ourselves than most of us realize. Hence, biofeedback 'demonstrates to us that our behaviour, as well as our physiology is pretty much our own doing' (Greenberg, 2008).

Bearing in mind the above, we realize that our psychological and physical wellbeing is often an issue under our control, as 'mind over matter', and therefore taking a break from a situation which is pulling us down, for example, by reading or enjoying a pleasant walk, can give us the opportunity to 'restart the engines'. By being able to detach ourselves from the stressful moments of our lives, we are then able to regain energy for leisure time and be better equipped to face the challenges of the next day with greater optimism and emotional strength, which is discussed below.

EMOTIONAL COPING TECHNIQUES

In addition to emphasizing the need to take control, this chapter would not be complete if we did not highlight the various coping strategies in relation to emotional techniques. One may certainly suggest that there is a close link between our emotional state and the way we interpret and react to our emotions and our physiological wellbeing – that is, how our bodies may react. Therefore, one could also suggest that the title of this book, *The Economic Crisis and Occupational Stress*, has as its underpinnings two meanings: first, that all crises are negative, and secondly that negative events give rise to negative emotions and feelings, such as disappointment, alarm and anger. The results, therefore, of such negativities can be seen at the individual level, organizational level and societal level – and this is currently evident across most countries around the globe.

Admittedly, it is often the meaning that we attribute to such negative events that becomes important and in recent years much has been written about the significance of our emotions. According to Weinberg et al. (2010), one established approach that helps to provide insight into how we comprehend our own and others' emotions is the concept of emotional intelligence (EI). This is 'the capacity to understand and harness for largely positive purposes, emotions experienced by ourselves and others' (cited in Weinberg et al., 2010). Indeed, US psychologist Daniel Goleman proposes that EI consists of four emotional and social competencies, which form the basis for our communications and functioning in a range of settings, including work and personal relationships (Goleman, 2000):

1. *Self-awareness*: the recognition of one's own emotions and their impact on others; the ability to identify and appraise one's strengths and weaknesses and possess a sense of self-confidence.
2. *Self-management*: covers a range of abilities which enable us to keep control over our feelings, to build trust with others, to be conscientious and flexible while focusing on attaining our goals and demonstrating initiative.
3. *Social awareness*: the capacity for sensing and gaining insight into the emotional circumstances of others, supporting them in their own development, identifying and meeting others' expectations and understanding the prevailing climate.
4. *Relationship management*: demonstrating successful social skills across settings which require sound two-way communication, persuasiveness, leadership, and the ability to handle conflict, promote change and teamwork (Weinberg and Cooper, 2010).

Although there is some disagreement about the extent to which these insights are reflections of our personalities and/or skills which can be learned, there is a growing body of evidence that points to the importance of emotional intelligence for a range of positive outcomes. The relevance of emotional intelligence is clearly elevated in difficult times, as increased levels of expressed emotions demand acknowledgement and responses, and hence there is a great need during economic and financial collapse to ensure that all emotions, of various states, are managed successfully. Simultaneously, there is also a need to understand the needs and emotions of others who also are fully immersed in these fast-moving turbulent times. Such changes will certainly be present in the working environment too, and there is therefore an ever greater need to fully acknowledge, understand and respect all employees' viewpoints. In other words, one should be able to reflect on the fundamental principles of emotional intelligence, especially during vulnerable periods of our lives.

FROM STRESS TO INDIVIDUAL, ORGANIZATIONAL AND SOCIETAL WELLBEING

Given the information that we have provided to readers in this final part of this book, we feel it is now necessary to pose the question 'Where do we go from here?' The answer is simple, and yet appears to be a double-edged sword: on the one hand, we are in a position to give recommendations on how the individual and organization should proceed in order to achieve improved wellbeing – and our advice is to closely observe and adhere to what we have written in these previous two chapters, as some of the recommendations will be applicable to you. However, it is almost impossible to predict with confidence how the world economy is likely to unfold in years to come. We may suggest (as we have written in Part I of this book), that our past is often an indicator of our future, as history acts as a pointer. With that in mind, world economies have both peaks and troughs, as all world economies and states of affairs appear to move in cyclical patterns. Therefore the likelihood of emerging from this worldwide recession, and in the very near future, is highly probable and we are optimistic that recovery is in sight. On the other hand, we also believe that lessons from this past should also be learnt – and as the ancient Greeks told the world many, many years ago, 'a fool is a fool if they make the same mistake twice'. Given, therefore, that we have experienced immense difficulties, economically, psychologically and socially, we believe that our road has now been mapped for us and we must follow the path with caution and steadiness. Here we must always remember human errors that have been made, and that corrections are needed to rectify the *human damage* that we have created. Thus, only by learning from our mistakes can we possibly move forward in a healthy and prosperous manner. Furthermore, it is necessary that both academics and practitioners work together on vitally important issues, as the areas and expertise of each and every scientist are essential to 'restart the propellers' and reach healthy and happy standards for all.

CONCLUSION

Looking on the Bright Side of Life

The famous old saying, 'always look on the bright side of life', is therefore simplistic and yet so true. With light at the end of the tunnel, an essential part of any coping regime is that we install *hope* in ourselves and others. However, hope is a varied term, with many different and personal meanings for each and every one of us. Hope can mean a small ray of hope and sunshine, which can be introduced by an expression of positive emotions, such as having small things to look forward to like a day by the sea or a walk in the park; this clearly serves a purpose and also takes us away from the constant need to be close to consumption, shops and shopping centres. Small rays of hope serve the purpose of encouraging small engagement with others, providing us with a platform for mutual support and encouragement with others. Perhaps one of the most important consolations is that in difficult times we tend to be like a pack of animals and we have a need to be together and join forces. Part of the emotional journey that we have all witnessed and experienced in this six-year global recession is that we are not alone – and so being with others in good and bad times is part of a human basic instinct and need. Having the opportunity to be together provides us with psychological security and strength that we all need in order to persevere. We must also remember that the human being is resilient, and we have an immense capacity to cope in difficult times, which has been seen in the most horrific atrocities carried out in history, when being together and united provides the emotional harnesses we all need.

In conclusion, therefore, we are of the opinion that life includes a series of challenges – and these challenges need to be met and mastered. Only through joining forces, understanding and learning from each other as well as learning and understanding the self, can we begin to face and overcome the challenges that have been set for us. Once we have accomplished this, we will all be in a stronger and better position to move forward into a new era of post-economic crisis which will encapsulate us moving from emotional and psychological sustainability to wellbeing and prosperity.

REFERENCES

Cooper, C.L., Flint-Taylor, J. and Pearn, M. (2013). *Building Resilience for Success*. Basingstoke: Palgrave Macmillan.

Dewe, P.J., O'Driscoll, M.P. and Cooper, C.L. (2010). *Coping with Work Stress*. Oxford: Wiley-Blackwell.

Fotinatos, R.S.J. (1996). Doctoral thesis, *A Community Wide Survey of Occupational Stress*. Manchester: UMIST.

Fotinatos-Ventouratos, R.S.J. and Cooper, C.L. (1998). Social class differences and occupational stress. *International Journal of Stress Management*, 5 (4), 211–22.

Goleman, D. (2000). Intelligent leadership. *Executive Excellence*, 3, 17.

Greenberg, J.S. (2008). *Comprehensive Stress Management*. 10th edn, New York: McGraw Hill.

Kassin, S., Fein, S. and Markus, H.R. (2011). *Social Psychology*. 8th edn. Belmont, CA: Wadsworth Cengage.

Kobasa, S. (1979). Stressful life events, personality, health: An enquiry into hardiness. *Journal of Personality and Social Psychology*, 37, 1–11.

Lazarus, R. and Folkman, S. (1984). *Stress, Appraisal and Coping*. New York: Springer Publications.

Lundberg, U. and Cooper, C.L. (2011). *The Science of Occupational Health: Stress, Psychobiology and the New World of Work*. Chichester: Wiley Blackwell.

Palmer, S. and Cooper, C.L. (2010). *How to Deal with Stress*. London: Kogan Page.

Rosseau, D. (1989). Psychological and implied contracts in organizations. *Employee Responsibilities and Rights Journal*, 2, 121–39.

Rosseau, D. (1995). *Psychological Contracts in Organizations: Understanding Written and Unwritten Agreements*. Thousand Oaks, CA: Sage.

Siegrist, J. (2009). Job control and reward: Effects on wellbeing. In S. Cartwright and C.L. Cooper (eds), *Oxford Handbook of Organizational Wellbeing*. Oxford: Oxford University Press, pp. 109–32.

Tuomilehto, J., Lindstrom, J., Eriksson, J.G. et al. (2001). Prevention of type 2 diabetes mellitus by changes in lifestyle among subjects with impaired glucose tolerance. *New England Journal of Medicine*, 344 (18), 1343–50.

Weinberg, A. and Cooper, C.L. (2012). *Stress in Turbulent Times*. Basingstoke: Palgrave Macmillan.

Weinberg, A., Sutherland, V.J. and Cooper, C.L. (2010). *Organizational Stress Management: A Strategic Approach*. Basingstoke: Palgrave Macmillan.

Yu, S., Yarnell, J.W.G., Sweetnam, P.M. and Murray, L. (2003). What level of physical activity protects against cardiovascular death? The Caerphilly study. *Heart*, 89, 502–506.

Index

absenteeism and working days lost 35, 83–4, 87
Africa 27
apathy 85–6
appraising threats 47
Asia 27, 70–71
austerity 23
Australia 18
Austria 18, 39, 41
autonomy *see* control factors
awareness 114, 124, 129, 132

Bank of America 61, 62
banking 4
  banking runs 21
  overleverage 13–14
  temporary work contracts 61, 62
Barber, Brendan 42, 57
Belgium 18
  unemployment (2001–2011) 38
    youth (2009–2011) 41
biofeedback 131
borrowing *see* debt
Brazil 19
Bulgaria 38, 41, 63
bullying and violence 36, 43–4, 46
Burke, R.J. and C.L. Cooper (2008) 60
burnout and reduced social interaction 85–6

Canada 18, 59, 84
car sales 79
challenge 47, 127, 134
change 5, 6–7, 61, 103, 127
  reviewing the psychological contract 41, 128–9
  see also uncertainty and insecurity
China 6, 17–18, 69, 79
cognitive-behavioural approach 114, 115
commitment 127

communication and information 44–5, 107–8, 109–10, 112
competitiveness and advantage 26
  global competition 52–3
  workforce reduction and 66, 89
confirmative biases 30–31
construction companies 90
consumerism and on-demand culture 61, 65
control factors 42–3, 107, 123, 125–6, 127
  self-awareness, self-management 124, 129, 132
  trade unions' role 60
Cooper, Professor Cary L. vi
  (2013) 113
  Burke, R.J. and (2008) 60
  Fotinatos-Ventouratos, R. and (1998) 43, 46, 107
  Lundberg, U. and (2011) 130
  Weinberg, A. and (2012) 7–8, 115–17
  Worrall, L. and (2012) 69, 80, 85–6, 101, 106–7, 111
coping strategies 113–18
  emotional techniques 132–3
  fitness programmes for strain symptoms 116–17
  hope 122, 134
  individual and organizational responsibilities 117–18
  objectivity 123
  physical wellbeing 129–30
  positive versus negative approaches 122–3
  relaxation time 130–31
  resilience, resistance and stamina 126–8
  reviewing the psychological contract 128–9
  self-appraisal 124, 129, 132
  self-management 132

self respect 123–5
social awareness 132, 134
stress management techniques
    113–14
symptom awareness 114
coping, the term 121–2
coronary heart disease 116–17, 130
costs of stress 76–95
    financial 5–6, 35, 84, 87–8, 108
    ill-health *see* health issues, causes
        and costs
    lifestyle choices 81
    organizational level 87–90
    societal level 90–93
        political and social unrest 54, 79,
            91–2
        reluctance to interact 85–6
        social provision 78
        unemployment rates 38–9, 41
    summary 93–5
crime 7–8
crises *see* economic crises model;
    economic crisis (2008)
Croatia 39
Cyprus 38, 41
Czechoslovak Republic 38, 41

debt 18
    affecting investment 76
    borrowing triggering crises 21–2
    default and rescheduling 22, 24, 25,
        27–9
    euro deficit data 55
    lack of state transparency 22–3
    sovereign external debt 22, 29
    willingness and ability to repay 23–4
demographics 61
Denmark 18, 85
    unemployment (2001–2011) 38
        youth (2009–2011) 41
Dewe, P.J. 102–3
distributional imbalance of wealth 26
DRAG (Deficit Reduction Anaemic
    Growth) 54

economic crises model 20–31
    avoidance (history repeating itself)
        22–4, 26, 30–31
    competitiveness and self-interest 26
    components 20–21

confirmative biases factor 30–31
Great Depression (1930s) 23, 117–18
    political and psychosocial
        considerations 23–4
    prevailing triggers 21–2
    productivity issues and monopolies
        30
    repetitive debt default and
        rescheduling 24–9
economic crisis (2008)
    origins 11–19
        cumulative tally of default and
            rescheduling 24–9
        failure to act 26
        mortgage meltdown and debt
            12–14, 76
    psychological impact of 3–4, 37
        in China 17–18
        in Europe 14–17
        work morale 46
    recovery claims 92–3
Economic Research and Investment
    Strategy 92
Economist Intelligence Unit 55–6
Egypt 22, 23
Einstein, Albert 65
emotional coping techniques 132–3
emotional intelligence 132
Employee Assistance Programmes
    (EAP) 118
employment changes *see* work changes
employment contracts 61, 92
empowerment 42–3, 107, 123
    trade unions' role 60
engagement surveys 113
Estonia 38, 41
euro crisis stressor 4, 8–9
    deficit and debt (2009–2012) 55
    foundational flaws 15–17, 22
    'rescue' packages 16
    troika negotiations 43
European Union 14–17, 87, 78–9
    debt default and rescheduling 25
    labour unit costs 15–16
    Maastricht Treaty 15
    social unrest 91–2
    unemployment (2001–2011) 38, 90,
        92
        youth (2009–2011) 41, 51–2, 66
    see also individual country names

European Agency for Safety and Health at Work 87
European Working Conditions Survey (2006) 5
expectations 40–41, 128

family issues *see* work–life imbalance
financial costs of stress 5–6, 35, 84, 87–8, 108
Finland 18, 39, 41, 46
fitness programmes 116–17
focus groups 113
Fotinatos-Ventouratos, Professor Ritsa vi
  Cooper, C.L. and (1998) 43, 46, 107
France 15, 78–9
  debt 18, 22
  unemployment (2001–2011) 38
    youth (2009–2011) 41

G-20 group of countries 12
Germany 15, 18, 78, 87
  unemployment (2001–2011) 38
    youth (2009–2011) 41
global affairs 78–9
global competition 52–3
global downturn 52–4
Goleman, Daniel 132
governments
  debt and transparency 22–3
    political and psychosocial factors 23–4
  regulation of work 52–5
  social provision 78
Great Depression (1930s) 23, 117–18
Greece 4–5, 16, 37, 84
  debt 18, 22
  social provision 78
  unemployment (2001–2011) 38, 76
    youth (2009–2011) 41

health issues, causes and costs
  and coping strategies 129–30
  mental 81–2
    absenteeism and cost to employer 83–4, 87
    reluctance to interact (burnout) 85–6

resignations and cost to employer 87–8
suicide rates 4–5, 78, 82
physical 46, 57, 77, 79–81
  heart disease and fitness programmes 116–17, 130
  metabolic syndrome 117
presenteeism 63, 84–5, 88–9
Holland 78
hope 122, 134
hours of work *see* working hours
Hungary 39, 41

identity 7
India 6, 19
individual and organizational frictions 51–73
  company actions
    costs and cutbacks 40–41
    restructuring and downsizing 44–5, 70
  costs of *see* costs of stress
  long hours culture 60–64
  macro factors (globalization and governments) 52–6
  producing 'symbolic' stressors 7
  managerial level 44–5, 67–9, 77, 79–80, 86, 106–7
  micro factors 56–64
    employee control issues 60
    family and childcare issues 61–2, 63, 66, 69–72
    increased performance assessment 68
    increased workloads 58–60, 65–6
    job insecurity effects 56–8
    longer work hours 42–3, 59
    drivers of 62–3
    short-lived employment contracts 61
  summary 72–3
  technological changes 64–7
  see also occupational stress; organizational effectiveness
individual wellbeing, future agenda 121–34
information and communication 44–5, 107–8, 109–10, 112
ING Bank, Netherlands 116

insecurity *see* uncertainty and insecurity
Inter-Heart Study 81
International Congress of Applied Psychology 113
International Labour Organization 89, 91
investment houses 13–14
Ireland 5, 15
    unemployment (2001–2011) 38
    and emigration 16
    youth (2009–2011) 41
Italy 15, 18, 63
    unemployment (2001–2011) 38
    youth (2009–2011) 41

Jahoda, Maria 7
Japan 18, 39, 59
job losses 44–5
Judge, Paul 68–9

Knapp, Jimmy 60
Kneale, Dennis 65
knowledge 44–5, 107–8, 109–10, 112

labour unit costs, Europe 15–16
Latin America 24, 25
Latvia 38, 41
leadership style 110–13
    employee/manager communication 109–10
    roles and relationships 108–9
Leahy, Terry 111
learning from history 20–31
Lithuania 38, 41
long hours culture 42–3, 59–64
Lundberg, U. and Cooper, C.L. (2011) 130
Luxembourg 38, 41

Maastricht Treaty 15
macroeconomic factors *see* individual and organizational frictions
Malta, unemployment 39, 41
managerial stresses 77, 79–80, 106–7
    by employment level 86
    downsizing 44–5
    producing abrasive style 67–9
managerial supportive style 109–13
manufacturing 78

Medicash 59, 63
Merrill Lynch 61
metabolic syndrome 117
methodological issues 102–3
Montenegro 63
mortgage meltdown 12–14
Murrell, P. (1982) 30

negativity 122–3, 132
Nestlé 116
Netherlands 16, 18, 78, 87, 116
    unemployment (2001–2011) 39
    youth (2009–2011) 41
NICE (National Institute for Clinical Excellence) 87–8, 111
NICE (Non-Inflationary Continuous Expansion) 53–4
Norway 18, 39

objectivity and psychological hardiness 123, 126–7
occupational stress 35–49
    appraising threats 47
    assessment (21st century) 48–9
    bullying and violence 36, 43–4, 46
    costs of *see* costs of stress
    early research into 36
    job insecurity 37, 56–8
    psychological strain 47–8
    working days lost through 35
    see also individual and organizational frictions
on-demand culture 61, 65
organizational causes of stress *see* individual and organizational frictions
organizational costs of strain 87–90
organizational effectiveness 101–18
    coping strategies (methodological issues) 102–3
    coping strategies (practical) 113–18
    fitness programmes for strain symptoms 116–17
    stress management techniques 113–14
    symptom awareness 114
    intervention strategies to maximize effectiveness 105–6
    supportive leadership style and strategies 110–13

valuing employees 11, 103–4, 117–18
workers' wellbeing, sustainability
    criteria 106–10
    '6-essentials' framework 108–9
    employee/manager
        communication 109–10
    see also individual and
        organizational frictions
organizational effects of stress *see*
    managerial stresses
Oxford Economics 5

part-time employment 92
pensions 7
performance assessment 68
Poland 39, 41, 61, 63
Portugal 18, 22, 37
    unemployment (2001–2011) 39
    youth (2009–2011) 41, 51
positivity 122–3
presenteeism 63, 84–5, 88–9
Primitive Production Function model
    11
problem-solving abilities 126
production input factors 11
productivity issues and monopolies
    30
psychological contract 41, 128–9
psychological hardiness and objectivity
    123, 126–7
psychological implications of economic
    crisis *see* coping strategies;
    economic crisis (2008); individual
    and organizational frictions;
    occupational stress
psychological strain 47–8
public disturbances 15, 54, 79, 91–2

Rational Emotional Therapy (RET)
    115
redundancy 44–5
relaxation techniques 130–31
reliance upon technical devices 64–7
Reinhard, C.M. and K.S. Rogoff
    (2003) 21, 26–7, 29
resilience and adaptability 48–9, 77,
    126–8, 134
Robertson, I.T. and J. Flint-Taylor
    (2009) 108–9
role conflict 108

Romania 23, 39, 41
Russia 19, 22

Sainsbury Centre for Mental Health 89
self-appraisal/self-awareness 124, 129,
    132
self-interest 26
self-management 132
self respect 123–5, 125
Simplyhealth 105, 108, 109, 110, 112
Slovenia 39, 41, 63
social awareness 132, 134
social interaction 85–6
social provision 78
societal strains, cost of 90–93
    global unemployment figures 38–9,
        41
    political and social unrest 15, 54, 79,
        91–2
    reluctance to interact 85–6
    social provision 78
South Korea 6
Spain 13, 15, 37, 61
    debt and bankruptcy 18, 22, 51, 90
    unemployment (2001–2011) 37, 38
    youth (2009–2011) 41
Spanish National Statistics Institute 90
strain 86
    coping with symptoms 116–17
    costs at organizational level 87–90
    costs at societal level 90–93
STRATFOR 51–2, 66, 78–9, 90
stress, costs of *see* costs of stress
stress, input and output dynamics 53
stress management *see* coping
    strategies
stressors *see* individual and
    organizational frictions;
    occupational stress; organizational
    effectiveness
suicide rates 4–5, 78, 82
The Sunday Times 'Best Companies to
    Work For' survey 103, 104, 106,
    111, 112
Sweden 18, 39, 41, 63, 84
'symbolic' stressors 7
symptom awareness 114

technological changes 64–7
temporary employment contracts 61

Terkel, Studs (1972) 3
'3Cs' 127
Towers Watson
    Global Workforce study 57, 58–9, 66
    Health, Wellbeing and Productivity
        study 70
trade union action 60, 79
Trade Union Congress 42, 57
training programmes 112
trust 69
Turkey 22, 23, 39

uncertainty and insecurity 36
    communicating bad news and 44–5
    health issues resulting from 46, 57
    job insecurity 37, 56–8
    re-employment strategies 124–5,
        128–9
    stress as threat or challenge 47, 127
    see also change
unemployment 11, 21, 49, 78–9
    global (2001–2011) 38–9
    percentage rates 4
    redundancy 44–5
    role of technological change 66–7
    seeking work strategies 124–5, 128–9
    youth 4, 16, 41–2, 51–2, 66–7
Unite 57
United Kingdom
    crime 7–8
    debt 18
    financial cost of stress 5–6
        resignation/replacement costs
            87–8
        through mental ill-health 84, 108
        unemployment rates and
            (2001–2011) 39
        youth (2009–2011) 41
        working days lost 35
    Foresight Project on Mental Capital
        and Wellbeing 68, 108
    Health and Safety Executive Board
        5, 45, 48, 106

social effects of crisis 15
    employment tribunals 67
    on family life 93
    health issues 57, 63, 68, 117
    increased workloads 58–9
    long work hours 42
    management stresses 77, 79–80,
        106–7
    trades reports and surveys 42
United States of America 12–14, 63,
    87
    abusive management 67
    debt 18
    employee wellbeing 107–8, 116
    export patterns (Murrell's
        hypothesis) 30
    Institute for Occupational Health
        and Safety 107
    new jobs 92
    unemployment (2001–2011) 39, 92
        (2013) 92

Weinberg, A. and C.L. Cooper (2012)
    7–8, 115–17
wellbeing *see* coping strategies
work changes 5, 6–7, 61, 103, 127
    reviewing the psychological contract
        41, 128–9
Work Foundation 42
work morale 46
work–life imbalance 61–4, 69–72
    pervasive technologies 64–7
workforce as key economic
    determinant 11
working days lost 35, 48
working hours 42–3, 59–64
    increase percentages 59
workloads 58–60, 65–6, 107
workplace, costs of strain 87–90
World Economic Forum 113
World Health Organization 5, 81, 105
Worrall, L. and C.L. Cooper (2012) 69,
    80, 85–6, 101, 106–7, 111